Major N F G Brehaut and Captain A D Stevens on the summit of Island
Peak (6189m) in the Himalayas, 1993.

# WE SUSTAIN

## THE ROYAL LOGISTIC CORPS
### 1993-1995

BY

## MICHAEL YOUNG

## Epilogue by HRH The Princess Royal

BARON
MCMXCV

PUBLISHED BY BARON BIRCH
FOR QUOTES LIMITED AND
PRODUCED BY KEY COMPOSITION,
SOUTH MIDLANDS LITHOPLATES, CHENEY & SONS,
HILLMAN PRINTERS (FROME),
AND WBC BOOKBINDERS

© The Royal Logistic Corps 1995

ISBN 0 86023 506 8

# CONTENTS

# FOREWORD _by Major General D L Burden CBE Director General Logistic Support (Army)_

## HEADQUARTERS QUARTERMASTER GENERAL
Portway Monxton Road Andover Hants SP11 8HT

Telephone Andover Military
(Direct Dialling) 0264 38 Ext 2998
(GTN Code) 1429
(Switchboard) 0264 382111
(Facsimile) Ext 2106

As I write it is nearly three and a half years since the Military Secretary, Lieutenant General Sir Willie Rous, now the Quartermaster General, informed me that I was to be the first Director General Logistic Support (Army) and to head the new Royal Logistic Corps. Over a year later, after months of meetings, visits, briefings and conferences and with the stately dance of military bureaucracy frequently interrupted by quick decisions, I waited with the 'Famous Five', the predecessor Directors General and Directors, for the arrival of our Colonel-in-Chief to take our formation parade. We looked at the driving rain from the Headquarters Mess, while down on the square a crowd including most of the Army Board sat stoically in the teeth of the gale; the signs were not auspicious! Miraculously the Royal helicopter arrived with a dramatic change in the weather, my own unspoken mood changed from pessimism to cautious optimism and the sun shone upon the parade and the raising of the new flag, a portent of good fortune that has continued to this day.

Recently a very senior officer of the Combat Arms said to me 'I cannot imagine the Army without The RLC. We are certain of you and you are at ease with yourselves' – a simple, meaningful compliment that is a tribute to the inspired example of a Colonel-in-Chief and her deputies, the support of the Colonels Commandant, the wisdom of the 'Famous Five', the hard work of the architects and executors of the Logistic Support Review, the commitment and imagination of our Regimental Headquarters staff and the professionalism of our officers and men. This book, full of stories of our immediate history through the formation period, pictures, anecdotes, humour, occasional sadness, humility and triumph, some mistakes, many successes, is not only an informal record of the early days of The Royal Logistic Corps but also a reflection of the contribution by many individuals to the creation of the largest Corps in the Army. It concentrates in one book much that would not be included in a formal history, and while it is fresh in the mind.

I hope that the selection of glimpses of Corps life will be equally appreciated by the serving and their predecessors and also be enjoyed by our friends in other parts of the Army and around the world. It is an informal record of a success story which belongs to all those involved.

_David Burden_

# INTRODUCTION *by Lieutenant Colonel Michael Young*

This book marks the turning of another page in the history of logistic support in the army, reflecting as it does the first two years of The Royal Logistic Corps, the official successor to the Royal Corps of Transport, Royal Army Ordnance Corps, Royal Pioneer Corps and Army Catering Corps, which Corps were amalgamated, and the Postal & Courier Service of the Royal Engineers, whose members were transferred to the new Corps.

The creation of The Royal Logistic Corps was an earthquake for the Forming Corps – views and reactions were of course varied, but change is as inevitable as the passing of time and, once our Masters in the Ministry had decided what to do, everyone had no choice but to get on with it and make the new organisation work. To think that there were no tears would be self-delusion, and there is the odd tear to be seen in these pages, but it would be a greater error not to think that enormous efforts have been made to build up an all-embracing sense of teamwork in the new Corps, often among those who had felt themselves previously to be rivals.

There is an overwhelming impression of that success in this book, which is amazing when the military society is traditionally considered to be opposed to change, and yet, when that change has been accepted, it handles it so well.

*We Sustain* is not a history book – it is far too early to be thinking of a history at this stage – although much of what appears here is undoubtedly of an historic nature. It is not a Corps *Journal* in hardback form – that would be a facile comment. If anything I like to think of it as a tapestry of the life of the Corps in its early times, with a miscellany of extracts from Corps *Journals* and contributions from units and individuals, none sure how the final product would look. The book's sole aim is to demonstrate in its own way the standing of a great Corps, of good people in that Corps, to illustrate that, although the Logistic Support Review was initiated for purely financial reasons, the result is a major success and a matter of considerable pride for all those involved.

There are five elements to *We Sustain*, four chapters variously giving a brief history of the Forming Corps, the formation of The Royal Logistic Corps and interesting extracts from a variety of letters and documents on regimental matters, impressions and contributions from units throughout the Corps, not forgetting a selection of photographs from my locked archive cupboard.

I would like to record my thanks to the Regimental Colonel, Colonel C M Lake, whose idea it was to incorporate letters from Regimental files, and the Regimental Secretary, Lieutenant Colonel J G Hambleton MBE, who made the selections, the Acting Curator, Mr Frank O'Connell, for selecting the historic photographs, and all units and individuals who contributed.

I am confident that those who were discerning, wise and courageous enough to subscribe to this book will enjoy it and give it an honoured place on their already groaning bookshelves.

# OUR PREDECESSORS: AN HISTORICAL PERSPECTIVE

The Royal Logistic Corps formed on 5 April 1993. Its acknowledged predecessors are the Forming Corps of the Royal Corps of Transport, Royal Army Ordnance Corps, Royal Pioneer Corps, Army Catering Corps and the Postal and Courier Service of the Royal Engineers. While each predecessor traces its own specific history variously to the 18th, 19th and 20th centuries, they all have antecedents which stretch back to the first use of men as soldiers in war. Today, as before, they have one task in common: the support of the British Army in peace and war, wherever it serves throughout the world.

In the early days, the army consisted solely of infantry and cavalry. In exchange for holding land and titles, the aristocracy provided the King with a quota of mounted knights and foot soldiers; armies were raised for particular campaigns and disbanded at their conclusion. An army consisting of infantry and cavalry alone, however, would not survive more than a day or two without administrative support and early records show that at least the lords and masters were kept in the style to which they had been accustomed. King Henry V's army had a 'Sergeant of the Waggons of the Household' during his Crecy campaign of 1415 in France, with even a 'Master of the Baggage Train' in 1422. Henry's army had some 25,000 horses and 'many carts and waggons', a huge organisation for those days. There was a 'Master of the Ordnance' who supplied war material as well as being the King's military treasurer and paymaster, the first officially recorded holder of the appointment being a Nicholas Merbury in 1414, with his headquarters in the Tower of London. The pay and muster rolls of the British garrison in Calais in 1346 show Pioneers receiving wages of between 4d and 6d a day. In contrast to their masters, the common soldiers lived by plunder, often as individuals, sometimes as units. At the end of each day, soldiers went in search of food and wood with which to cook it. Later an officers' party moved ahead or to the flank of an army to procure its food and wood, to await the main body's arrival. The disadvantages of the plunder system were essentially that the army was a disorganised rabble while it was looking after itself; there was also little or no cooperation between the army and the civilian population, indeed, there was no food or help in the event of a withdrawal. The advantage of that system was that it was cheap, little or no transport was needed and no food needed to be supplied. Campaigning was generally a summer occupation when food was readily available.

Interestingly it was when a woman, the Tudor Queen Elizabeth, wore the Crown, that the necessity for feeding soldiers from government sources began to be recognised and the titles 'Proviant-Master-General' and 'Waggon-Master-General' appear. The Proviant-Master-General was responsible for 'providing victuals, corn, flesh, wine, bread and beer; for inspecting them; and issuing them to units according to their strengths'; he was also responsible for the stocking of garrisons and fortifications with all forms of non-perishable foodstuffs, fuel and forage, and for all forms of live edible beasts and birds. Answerable to the Treasury, he was provided with a Lieutenant, a clerk, blacksmith, waggon-master, quartermaster and a number of 'Directors'. The Ordnance Office, later to become the Board of Ordnance, provided technical support and materiel to line regiments. The Board's agents, the Commissaries of Ordnance, supplied all manner of 'warlike stores' with the vital technical and scientific developments in small arms, artillery and ammunition emerging from the laboratories and arsenal at Woolwich. Arms and ammunition for the Royal Navy were also supplied by the Board of Ordnance, in addition to the fortifications and accommodation in every outpost of the Empire. As the business of warfare became increasingly scientific, the formation and control of the Corps of Engineers and Artillery became an additional responsibility of the Master General of Ordnance. He held an important political post too, in that he was adviser to King and Parliament on military

Incident at Hougoumont Farm during the Battle of Waterloo 18 June
1815. A Royal Waggon Train tumbril arrives at Hougoumont Farm,
having driven through heavy enemy fire to deliver desperately needed
ammunition to the 3rd Guards (later the Scots Guards). The arrival of this
ammunition saved the day. Painting by Charles Stadden.

matters. Later great military leaders such as the Dukes of Marlborough and Wellington held the post.

The Waggon-Master-General oversaw the movement of the armys baggage and stores, being responsible for the waggon train, its order of march and its discipline directly to the Generals commanding the Horse and Foot respectively. With the control of supplies under the Treasury, control of transport under the army and control of ordnance under Parliament the efficiency of the army was inevitably to suffer from inter-departmental conflict and personal influence, a matter which was eventually to be better regulated at the end of the 19th century. Only gradually were organisations such as the Commissariat, formed in 1645, and the Barrack-Master-General, whose office dates from 1699, incorporated in the mainstream of the military arm, but several centuries of experience and constant reorganisations were needed before this was achieved. The Commissariat initially only comprised financial agents providing money and negotiating contracts for the army, but in campaigns they bought stocks in anticipation of future needs and so became holders of stores. As agents of the Treasury, Commissariat officers were influential and independent, not always to the army's advantage.

During the Civil War of the 1640s both the Royalist and Roundhead armies survived largely on requisition and acquisition, with no Commissariat magazines or transport available. The effect of transport and supply on the war was minimal – both sides were well-fed and moved largely on foot, in their own country, supported by their own sides. With the arrival of Cromwell's Commonwealth, however, there appeared in 1645 the New Model Army, the first recognizable forerunner of the army as we know it today, an army of 22,000 all ranks organised into twelve Regiments of Foot. The army had a headquarters and staff, and a Commissary of Victuals issued a ration of bread and cheese to the troops – the first ration scale was in fact authorised in 1689. Commissariat transport, much of it hired, carried rations, ammunition and the sick and wounded. The Artillery and Engineers had their own waggon trains under the Board of Ordnance, which itself was also responsible for the procurement of artillery and other ordnance.

The Duke of Marlborough, in command of an allied army campaigning against the French in Europe, was determined to end the plunder system and ordered the Commissariat to provide meat twice a week for the soldiers, although they had to pay for the pleasure. With his far-seeing administrative arrangements, the Duke was perhaps the first great commander to provide well for his army, but the successful conclusion to his campaigning after Blenheim led to his organisation being dismantled in 1713.

It was not until the Duke of York raised an army to fight in Flanders that the Royal Corps of Waggoners was authorized by Royal Warrant on 7 March 1794: some 500 men under the command of Captain James Pool, to operate under the Commissariat. At the same time a Corps of Artillery Drivers was raised, under the control of the Ordnance Board. With poor quality soldiers and no effective leadership the transport organisation fared badly, but no worse than the rest of the campaign. On their return to England in 1796 the Waggoners were disbanded. What is important, however, about this brief interlude is that the Royal Corps of Waggoners were the first transport and supply body organic to the British Army, *ie* not hired or acquired; their lack of success was clearly not as disastrous as might appear, since another transport organisation was established in 1799 for an expedition to the Low Countries under the command of Sir Ralph Abercrombie, the Royal Waggon Corps, which in 1802 changed its name to the Royal Waggon Train.

Having formed in Bromley, Kent under the command of Lt Col Digby Hamilton, a friend

ABOVE: Commissariat difficulties in the Crimea 1854-56. BELOW:
Rorke's Drift, 1879. Painting by C C P Lawson.

of the Prince Regent, with five companies of 100 men each, the depot of the Royal Waggon Train moved to Croydon and expanded in numbers. Its Band, which is said to have included blackamoors, was extremely popular with local people on their walks around the barrack area and in local parks.

The Royal Waggon Train, although small, did sterling work in Spain, supporting Wellington's army in his campaign against Napoleon's marshals. Conditions tested the organisation to the full, with huge distances to cover and sometimes appalling weather conditions, not to mention unreliable sources and uncooperative Spaniards. The Commissariat controlled much more transport, with some 400 bullock carts and 12,000 pack animals, and there was the Artillery Field Train too, which conveyed and issued ordnance in the field and supervised the movement of guns.

Communication between the seat of government and an army in the field is an essential for coordinated military success and in this matter the army in Spain was well-served, in spite of the distances involved. A weekly ship from Falmouth to Lisbon delivered official mail as well as private correspondence, of which there was relatively little, since most soldiers could not read or write. Mail passed to the Quartermaster General, who had two Sergeant Postmasters, but the service was difficult and unreliable, especially since recipients had to pay the postage costs.

After the Battle of Waterloo in 1815 French domination of Europe came to an end and the British Army was largely dissipated or disbanded. The Royal Waggon Train, having been awarded the battle honours 'Peninsula' and 'Waterloo', was disbanded in 1833 as part of a major reduction in the size of the army. Wellington wrote in 1816 of the Train: 'No person can be more impressed than I am of the necessity of a corps of the description of the Royal Waggon Train, and I am perfectly sensible of the exertions made, and the expenses incurred to complete the Corps at the Commencement of the last war. But the

total failure of all those exertions and expenses to produce anything that was not a disgrace to the Service shows that some measure should be adopted in time-of-peace in order to have for service a corps so necessary in time of war'. Sadly, words of wisdom spoken in times of war are invariably ignored in times of peace

The next British military involvement was in 1854, in the Crimea, when Britain and France fought Russia and Turkey, with the Commissariat alone still responsible for contracting out the logistic support of the army, although that separate department, the Ordnance Board, still operated its Field Train in support of artillery and engineer units. Each man arrived in the Crimea with one blanket, three days' pork and biscuit, but no tentage; there was no regimental transport, no supply system and the bad weather caused unimaginable hardship. A much reduced Commissariat was expected to support a force of 33,000 men with only 75 mules and a few carts – and instructions from the Treasury to operate as cheaply as possible.

Despite their Herculean efforts the army's administration was a disaster and health and morale were at a low ebb. It took a public outcry in Britain, largely caused by Russell's dispatches in *The Times* and the fall of the government, to effect the transfer of the Commissariat from the Treasury to the Horse Guards, the formation of a Hospital Conveyance Corps for the sick and wounded, and the formation, in January 1855, of the Land Transport Corps under its Director-General, Colonel W M S McMurdo. The Board of Ordnance was disbanded in 1855.

This new Corps was charged 'with the Land Transport of all stores, supplies and necessaries at all times required by Our Army in the Field'. Raised largely in London (the Wellington Arms, 162 Waterloo Road), the Corps was classed as cavalry and divided into two wings, each intended to alternate as echelons on different days. Each wing comprised six divisions, one for each division of the Expeditionary Force, with a total of

ABOVE: Army Service Corps transport near Mafeking, c1900. BELOW: Army Ordnance Corps at an Artillery Camp in Glen Emaal, Ireland in 1904.

13

some 48 officers, 2,270 British soldiers and 5,800 natives, and a carrying capacity of 19,200 mule loads. This organisation soon changed, but for the first time supply was allocated to formations. It was also the first time that railways were used to support the army: civilian engineers constructed a railway at Balaclava. Where slopes were too steep for the engines, the Land Transport Corps hitched its horses to the waggons for pulling power.

Mail to the Crimea was a civilian responsibility and the French post office system was used, though clerks were obtained from the military to help with sorting and unit identification. Later, ships of the Royal Navy were used, but this proved even more unreliable. Some two million letters passed between UK and the Crimea and the postal organisation was hard-pressed. Payment by the recipient was still a problem.

Following the war, close links between the army and the Post Office were formed and, after unfruitful recommendations to convert the 49th Middlesex Rifle Volunteers to a Postal Corps in 1877, a Royal Warrant dated 22 July 1882 authorised the formation of the Post Office Corps to be formed by the 24th Battalion Middlesex Volunteers for service in the Egyptian and Sudanese campaigns. Four Senior NCOs, four Corporals and thirty-five men embarked for Egypt, making a promising start under difficult circumstances. It was during the Sudan campaign to save General Gordon in Khartoum that the first official link was made with the Royal Engineers, since it was their telegraphy service that was used. History is full of humour: commenting on the postal services, a newspaper recounted an incident when the postal launch carrying mail from Ismailia to Port Said ran into a torpedo boat and sank. The poor postal launch was awarded the blame!

The Crimea provided the first occasion when the army started to look seriously at catering. Whereas food in units was prepared by those who were 'blessed with some culinary talent or who were failing in any other skill', the introduction of the Soyer Boiler, the design of Alexis Soyer, did at least initiate a mobile form of cooker to provide hot food for the soldier from a central, regimental source. This was followed by the development for training camps at home of the 'Aldershot Oven' which saw service into the Second World War. It was in 1870 that Sergeant Cooks were authorised in all regiments of the army; and in 1883 a major advance was achieved by the creation in Salamanca Barracks, Aldershot of the first Instructional Kitchen. It may have been only a small school, which trained Messing Officers, but no cookery training had taken place in the army before that. Command Cookery Schools, the next development, were set up by the Army Service Corps before the Great War 1914-18, and these were responsible for cookery training in the army until 1941

Following the Crimean War, the Land Transport Corps was replaced in 1856 by the Military Train, consisting of seven battalions, one for each division. The Train was fully combatant and ranked in Army Lists after the most junior cavalry regiment. Since many of its soldiers had transferred from cavalry regiments they were only too happy not to be employed in transport and supply roles in the two overseas campaigns for which the Land Transport Corps is well-known, the Indian Mutiny and the New Zealand Maori Wars.

It was at Azimghur outside Lucknow in April 1858 that Privates Murphy and Morley of the 2nd Battalion Military Train were each awarded the Victoria Cross, and when the battalion left Calcutta at the end of its tour, a special congratulatory order was issued and a salute of guns fired. The Military Train earned the battle honours 'Lucknow' and, from subsequent service in China, 'Taku Forts' and 'Pekin'.

The period from the end of the 1860s is complicated and any full account would be unreadable. In outline, however, a Control Department was formed in 1869, an officer corps designed to control a supply and transport sub-department. The Army Service Corps was the major component, along with the Military Stores Staff Corps which had

ABOVE: A Travelling Post Office in France, 1918. BELOW: Labour
unloading stones for road repair, France, 1917.

been formed in 1865 by Royal Warrant. An officer-only Military Store Department meanwhile had formed in 1861. On formation, the Army Service Corps consisted of twelve transport companies and ten supply companies, with No 1 (Depot) Company based at Aldershot. Following the examples of the Land Transport Corps and Military Train, the uniform was dark blue, with two white stripes. In 1876 the Control Department was split up and replaced by a Commissariat and Transport Department, an Ordnance Store Department and a Pay Sub-department, all under a Surveyor-General of Ordnance in the War Office. Although the title of the officers changed back to Commissaries, the status and organisation of the Army Service Corps remained unchanged. In 1877 the Ordnance Store Companies of the Army Service Corps were separated from the supply and transport units and concentrated at Woolwich under the Ordnance Store Branch of the Army Service Corps.

During the Zulu War of 1879 the Commissariat and Transport Department had in its ranks Assistant Commissary James Dalton. He was awarded the Victoria Cross for his outstanding bravery at Rorke's Drift in January 1879, and Corporal Attwood of the Army Service Corps was awarded the Distinguished Conduct Medal for his spirited defence of the hospital.

In January 1880 the Commissariat and Transport Department was redesignated the Commissariat and Transport Staff. Officers of this Corps commanded Army Service Corps companies until August 1881 when the Army Service Corps became the Commissariat and Transport Corps. There were two main depots where its personnel were trained: Aldershot for Horse Transport and Supply, and Woolwich for Horse Transport. The Ordnance Store Companies went to a new Ordnance Store Corps, later to become part of the Royal Army Ordnance Corps.

General Sir Redvers Buller VC became Quartermaster General in 1887 and used his experience in Africa and Canada and advice from the last of the Commissary Generals, Sir

Edward Morris, to create a second Army Service Corps in 1888, insisting that, for the first time since the Peninsular War, transport and supply units should be staffed by combatant officers of high calibre, wearing the same uniform and badges as their men. As an early sign of changing times the first logistic officer to go to the Staff College was Major R H L Warner ASC in 1894.

Meanwhile the Quartermaster General's office in Whitehall was less interested in the world of Ordnance since stores and munitions were not perceived as an everyday requirement, and unnecessary holdings were expensive. Ordnance officers did not hold combatant commissions and were not eligible for staff appointments; their technical skills, considerably in excess of other regimental officers, were smothered and frustrated in the army inefficiency of the day. In 1896, however, reforms were adopted which imposed a form of rationalization in storekeeping and accounting, improved training, pay and ordnance matters, as well as amalgamating five branches into an Army Ordnance Department and Corps. These branches were the Ordnance Store Department and four Inspectorates (General Stores, Warlike Stores, Small Arms and Guns). This reorganisation was largely the work of a brilliant administrator, Colonel John Steevens, who was later to become the first Colonel Commandant of the Royal Army Ordnance Corps. While improving the position of Ordnance within the United Kingdom, nothing was achieved in integrating the Army Ordnance Department into the field force organisation, which meant exclusion from mainstream involvment in the army as a whole. In essence, senior commands and staffs had not yet learnt or thought through how best to provide administrative support in peace and war. Also in 1896, collar badges incorporating elements of the arms of the old Board of Ordnance were brought into use.

After its experience in the Red River Expedition in Canada (1869-70), the Ashanti War (1873-74), the South African Wars of 1877-81, Egypt and the Sudan (1882-85) and a host of other campaigns in Africa, the Army

ABOVE: Army Service Corps horse transport in difficulties on the muddy roads of France, 1917. BELOW: Holt caterpillar tractor of the Army Service Corps pulls a heavy gun of the Royal Artillery alongside GS waggons during the 1914-18 war.

Service Corps was experienced and well-organised to support the army. Needless to say, the South African War of 1899-1902 posed problems of logistics of which the British Army had no experience – the lessons of the Peninsular War were long forgotten. The area of operations was vast and the means of communication poor. The total strength of the forces employed against the Boers, including colonial and irregular troops, peaked at 450,000 men. Virtually the entire Army Service Corps was sent to South Africa, over 3,000 men, as well as 1,000 men of the Army Ordnance Corps. The Army Service Corps formed the main transport links forward of the railheads, with companies split into two parts, and operated depots on the lines communication for food, forage and ammunition. Some 600 drivers were attached to the Royal Artillery to replace their casualties – included in their achievements was the recovery of two guns under heavy Boer fire at Colenso. With little experience in the field the Army Ordnance Corps improvised a supply for ordnance stores as the campaign developed, and surmounted bravely its most pressing difficulties. For its part in the war, the Army Service Corps was honoured in 1902 with the appointment of Queen Victoria's son, HRH The Duke of Connaught, as its Colonel (later Colonel-in-Chief).

The postal system got off to a shaky start on the outbreak of war in 1899, since little had changed since Wellington's campaigns. A Post Office Corps had been formed, followed by a second Army Postal Corps called the Royal Engineers Telegraph Reserve – both were reorganised into two supplementary companies. Sixty-three men left for South Africa in October 1899, with others to follow. The HQ and Base Post Office were established in Cape Town and Field Post Offices were set up in due course in the Cape and Natal.

Difficulties soon abounded: Captain Treble, the Army Postmaster, did not receive the assistance he needed from the Post Office and the War Office in the early months of the war and information on unit locations was hard to come by. Additionally there were problems of transport and security, but determination and dedication brought success before too long, assisted by 100 reinforcements in 1900. At the end of the war 630 officers and men had taken part, and 500,000 letters and newspapers as well as 12,000 parcels had been delivered to the troops each week. With the increase in the use of, and the improvements in, the railway the war also saw the introduction of Travelling Post Offices.

After the Boer War Field Post Offices were used increasingly on manoeuvres and it was agreed that the Army Postal Corps should continue as a reservist organisation, but this somehow got lost in the reorganisation of the Volunteer Army. In 1908, however, the new establishment of the Territorial Army contained provision for postal detachments in all fourteen Divisions and, after several years, the link with the Royal Engineers (as the Postal Section) was formalized, was published in 1913.

1911 saw the appointment of Lieutenant-Colonel G Morgan ASC as the first Messing Adviser in the Quartermaster General's department in the War Office. He was brought out of retirement for this task, but, alas, did not last a year. All the army was left with in the war was an Inspector of Catering, supported by Catering Instructors from a variety of regiments, under the Director of Supplies and Transport Branch of the Quartermaster General's Directorate.

In 1904 Lord Esher headed a committee which reorganised the structure of army control. Out of this came the Army Council (now the Army Board). The Quartermaster General became responsible for material and his Director of Equipment and Ordnance Stores became the Chief of Ordnance Services, which broke the command link to the Director of Artillery. His organisation was responsible for stores and the supply of clothing.

ABOVE: An Army Ordnance Department ammunition dump at Contay, France in 1917. BELOW: Sorting Ordnance stores at the dockside in France, 1918.

19

The post mortem after the Boer War equally affected the Army Service Corps and the responsibility for all mechanical transport in the army was allocated to that Corps, which initially took over a handful of steam engines from the Royal Engineers, who had operated them in South Africa. The principle was also established that the operator would repair his own equipment; the first MT workshop was established in Aldershot in 1905. Automobiles were purchased for use as staff cars from 1902 and 1903 saw the formation of the first mechanical transport unit, 77 Company ASC in Aldershot. With the world of steam and combustion engines developing fast, a number of transport companies soon came into being, but the horse still remained the main means of locomotion within the Division until after the Great War.

For the first time, too, Ordnance was represented in each Division, with a Deputy Assistant Director Ordnance Services (a Major) and a Staff Sergeant Major being responsible for all Ordnance Services. They were later given sufficient staff to deal with the flow of stores in Divisional HQ and within the Division. All this allowed for a better coordination of logistic support in the field.

When war was declared in August 1914 the Army Service Corps and Ordnance Services expanded enormously. Fortunately horses and transport had been incorporated into mobilization plans, so that a British Expeditionary Force of several Divisions was adequately supported; nevertheless the retreat from Mons towards Paris caused great losses, which were not easily replaced by a system which still saw no reason to stockpile ordnance material, clothing, saddlery and other necessities of war.

A Base Ordnance Depot was set up at Havre, with subsidiary depots at Rouen and Boulogne, and large ammunition dumps were established in the forward areas to ease the problem of resupply. Similarly the Army Service Corps had depots at Havre, Calais, Rouen and Abbeville. The routine system of supply was from the UK base, through a variety of ports to the continent, then from base depots to advanced depots; rail movement was used from the base to the depots on the continent, thence to a railhead. Divisional horse transport collected from railheads for distribution to units forward, with 3rd line mechanical transport responsible for the delivery of ammunition to the Heavy Artillery.

300 men of the Postal Section left immediately with the British Expeditionary Force for France on the outbreak of war, leaving only thirty in England. The Postal Home Depot remained in London (Mount Pleasant) but the enormous increase in mail caused it to be moved several times, including to Regents Park; in 1917, part of the work was diverted to main post offices, including Manchester, Leeds, Sheffield, Bristol, Birmingham and Glasgow. Mails for the continent were moved initially *via* Southampton to Havre, but later *via* Folkestone to Boulogne. As in previous wars security was a major problem, so that unit location information was scarce; the view was held in some quarters that mail was a luxury and should have no priority over supply ships, trains or transport columns. The use of Railheads and Refilling Points for mail was risky because of the changing tactical situation, so it was not long before independent transport was used and it was normal for mail to arrive in a forward trench two days after being posted in UK. Throughout the war postal staff had to battle constantly against lack of shipping space, unsympathetic planners and operational factors, but their determination, ingenuity and resourcefulness in providing a service of pin-point accuracy have to be admired. At the height of the war, over 7,000 men were employed, the Home Depot handled 2,000 million letters and papers, and moved 114 million parcels. The morale factor of an efficient postal service can never be underestimated.

The long period of static warfare in France and Belgium led to the expenditure of

ABOVE: Driver training at Feltham, 1926. BELOW: Army Post Office in
North Africa, 1941.

ammunition on an unprecedented scale. Mass production resulted in a heavy burden on the Army Ordnance Corps in the field of supply and storage; the inspection, repair of ammunition and other technical ammunition work were undertaken on a scale never attempted outside Woolwich Arsenal, and schools were necessarily established to train officers and NCOs to deal not only with all the new natures of ammunition produced during the war, but also with German ammunition.

Whereas the Army Service Corps was responsible for vehicle workshops the Army Ordnance Corps operated workshops for Artillery, including mobile workshops well forward. Wear and tear on the guns placed a tremendous strain on the technical staff who had to keep them in action.

Another major problem arose from the sheer size of the continental army – labour. For inloading/outloading depots and ports, as well as on the Lines of Communication, the Army Service Corps established Labour Companies in August 1914, each of some 530 men. The Royal Engineers and Ordnance Depots, too, soon required large amounts of labour; in 1915 calls were made on South Africa, the West Indies, China and India to supply personnel. In 1916 42,000 men were so employed and, when these figures rose even higher, a Labour Corps was established in January 1917, with a Labour Directorate in GHQ. At the end of the war in 1918, 124,000 men were employed in labour duties. Having made a considerable contribution to the war effort, the Labour Corps was disbanded in 1919 and it was not until 1939 that its need was felt again.

Teamwork, however, is the key to all success and each Corps had contributed enormously. The Army Ordnance Corps started the war with 240 officers and 2,300 men; during the war it expanded to 2,400 officers and 39,000 men. The Army Service Corps started with 500 officers and 6,000 men and finished with 10,400 officers and 315,000

men, as well as 23,800 cars and vans, 56,600 lorries and tractors and 34,000 motor cycles.

During the war Army Service Corps responsibilities expanded greatly to include the provision of fuel, including fuel tankers, vehicles and drivers for all HQs, medical units and non-Army Service Corps units, the Expeditionary Force Canteen and motor-cycle orderlies; all heavy guns of the Artillery were towed, Engineer pontoon parks transported and even Signal Section mobile pigeon lofts driven; 83,000 men were transferred to the infantry to replace casualties and in exchange for men of lower medical category, and over 100 officers transferred to the Royal Flying Corps.

Decorations and awards to members of all the Corps were many, but of particular importance are the Victoria Crosses awarded to 2nd Lt Alfred Herring ASC and Private George Masters ASC in 1918.

During 1918 experiments were carried out using modified aircraft for transporting the army's mail by air. As the tests proved successful, the first regular air service from Folkstone to Cologne was set up in March 1919, using RAF Handley Page aircraft to provide British troops in Germany with a fast mail service.

Abroad the Army Service Corps and Ordnance Services provided essential support, in Salonika, Gallipoli, East Africa, Mesopotamia, Egypt, Palestine, Italy and Russia. Each theatre produced its own problems and deserves its own account.

In recognition of their splendid work the title 'Royal' was granted on 25 November 1918 to the Army Service Corps, and to the Army Ordnance Department and Army Ordnance Corps on their amalgamation as the Royal Army Ordnance Corps.

In spite of large scale demobilization in 1919 the army still had commitments in many parts of the world, including the occupation of the Rhineland, which ended in 1929. The contraction to a peacetime footing hit everyone hard, not least because the country's

ABOVE: Pioneer Corps unloading supplies in Tobruk, 1942. BELOW:
Pioneer Corps men making a road on the Anzio Beach, 1944.

economy was bankrupt, a situation which was not helped by a world depression. The Postal Service remained with the British Army of the Rhine but otherwise it was largely reduced to Supplementary Reserve status.

The Royal Army Service Corps saw the further reduction of horse transport units as mechanization increased throughout the army, and Feltham was created as the first purely Mechanical Transport Station in peacetime, combining the Heavy Repair Shop from Hounslow, the Driving School from Bulford, the MT Stores Depot from Deptford and the Vehicle Reserve Depot. The Royal Army Service Corps took over responsibility for training all drivers throughout the army and the Royal Army Ordnance Corps was made responsible in 1929 for the supply, storage and repair of all non-RASC vehicles and other Arms' tracked and fighting vehicles. An experimental workshop was set up in Aldershot which, in the continuing quest for increased mobility, developed six–wheel trucks as well as tracked and wheeled tractors to pull medium and heavy guns. In the 1930s a new Divisional Column RASC was created, comprising an HQ, and Supply, Ammunition and Baggage Companies, each with its own mobile workshop section. Never had such a complete and adequate transport system been designed to support the British Army in the field. The Royal Army Service Corps and Royal Army Ordnance Corps provided units for a host of peacetime emergencies: Turkey in 1922, Shanghai in 1927, Palestine in 1930, the Saar in 1934, and the Western Desert as a result of the Italian invasion of Abyssinia.

After 1919 the Royal Army Ordnance Corps soon realised that Red Barracks, Woolwich were too cramped as the headquarters of the Corps and, with the Depot, School of Instruction and Record Office, moved to Hilsea near Portsmouth, where they remained until 1940. With increasing cuts and civilianization the Corps were driven back to the basic duty of providing the minimum needs of the army in peace, so that a static

organisation only developed, with no up-to-date, tested Field Force organisation and no Regular Field Force units in peace. Its non-combatant status (changed in 1941) again deterred progress.

In 1921 the Royal Army Ordnance Corps band was formed, 'recognised' but not 'authorised'. As with the Royal Army Service Corps, the officers paid for expenses incurred. The Corps March selected was *The Village Blacksmith*. The Royal Army Service Corps band had also been formed, unofficially in 1888, its march *Wait for the Waggon* dating from 1875, the occasion of a visit to Aldershot by the Sultan of Zanzibar. It, too, was eventually recognised officially, thus relieving the pockets of its officers of an unfair expense. The Pioneer Corps Regimental March was specially composed for the Corps in 1943, and the Corps March of the Army Catering Corps, *Roast Beef of Old England*, dates from 1947.

In the 1930s, catering in the army was the subject of considerable attention in a drive to improve standards of living for the soldier. In 1938 Sir Isidore Salmon, Chairman of Lyons, was invited by Mr Hore-Belisha, the Secretary of State for War, to become Honorary Advisor on army catering. In 1939 the new School of Army Cookery was built opposite Clayton Barracks, Aldershot, to replace the single block used in Buller Barracks since the end of the Great War. Civilian Catering Advisers were appointed in each of the Home Commands, and a new barracks, St Omer, the new School of Cookery, was set in train.

1938 saw the start of serious preparation for war as Prime Minister Chamberlain's influence on Hitler proved illusory. Militia men reported and the process of mobilization started. In 1939 the Territorial Army was embodied and National Service introduced; the 'impresssed vehicle' scheme was put into operation and an even larger range of vehicles was unceremoniously painted khaki than had been the case in 1914. Transport, Ordnance and Pioneer units came rapidly into being, the latter initially as the Auxiliary Military Pioneer Corps (changed a year later

ABOVE: A Royal Army Service Corps composite rations dump in
Tunisia, c1941. BELOW: Tank transporters on an autobahn in Germany,
1945.

25

to Pioneer Corps) and Britain again sent a British Expeditionary Force to France, only twenty-five years after its predecessor in 1914. The tactical and logistic situations were in many ways comparable, only this time the German Army was significantly more successful, causing in May and June 1940 the harried remnants of the British Army to be evacuated through Dunkirk as well as from areas further south. Many Corps soldiers were prisoners-of-war until 1945.

From Norway in 1940 to North Africa, Greece, Crete, Hong Kong, Malaya and Singapore, Burma, Malta, Italy to France, Belgium and Germany in 1944-45, the Second World War raged on. As ever, the British Army started badly but finished well.

On 22 March 1941 the Army Catering Corps was formed by Special Army Order 35, and the first Director was effectively Colonel R A A Byford, then Deputy Director Supplies and Transport, ST 4 (Catering) in the War Office. The first Commandant ACC Training Centre in the new St Omer Barracks, where the Corps formed, was Lieutenant-Colonel R Russell. Sir Isidore Salmon was followed in 1959 as Honorary Catering Adviser to the army by his nephew, Geoffrey Salmon, in turn succeeded in 1971 by his son, Harry Salmon. During the war the Corps became a highly successful organisation. Included were a great number of civilian catering experts called up for the duration. Some 70,000 officers and men served in the Army Catering Corps during the war. On 5 October 1945 the Army Council took the decision to retain the Corps as an integral part of the post-war army.

Pioneers performed a wide variety of tasks in the UK and in every theatre of war, having recruited in East and West Africa, Swaziland, Basutoland, Bechuanaland, Mauritius and India. Companies established with Beach Groups took part in the assaults in North Africa, Sicily, Italy and North-West Europe – on D Day twenty-six Companies, totalling 7,500 men, landed on the Normandy beaches. By D+60 they were followed by thirty-four Group HQs and a further 205 Companies –

60,000 men. They worked on the beaches, laid prefabricated track, handled all types of stores and ammunition and carried out stretcher-bearing and road-making duties. With Engineer supervision other Companies built the Mulberry Harbour, laid the Pipe Line Under the Ocean (PLUTO), constructed airfields and erected bridges. Strategic and tactical smoke screens were laid by Pioneers, who also supplied the smoke cover for the crossing of the Rhine.

At most operational ports and railheads, Pioneers were responsible for all non-technical labour, but they were often able to take over technical tasks without supervision. Companies were trained to fight and took their place in the line as infantry in Tunisia. Less spectacular, but nevertheless essential, were the Lines of Communication and Base tasks performed overseas and in the UK. Millions of tons of stores were handled for the Services at all stages of transit. Pioneers became expert in loading and unloading railway wagons and motor transport.

Pioneer and Civil Labour Units (PCLUs) recruited civilians as close to the fighting as possible, so relieving the strain on the military Pioneer. These units were particularly successful in recruiting skilled artisans and clerks for the Royal Engineers, Royal Army Ordnance Corps and Royal Electrical & Mechanical Engineers units, as well as a large number of unskilled workers.

It was an enormous, worldwide commitment which may be fairly judged from the fact that in 1945 the Pioneer Corps included 12,000 officers and controlled the following numbers of men:166,000 uniformed Pioneers, 330,000 labourers from a variety of countries in the Empire, 1,074,000 civilian labour and 173,000 prisoner-of-war labour officered and staffed by the Pioneer Corps, a grand total of 1,743,000. Many decorations for gallantry were gained by officers and soldiers of the Corps, one being Corporal J P Scully who was awarded the George Cross on 8 July 1941, one of the first.

The Postal Section of the Royal Engineers was authorised on 24 August 1939, just ten

ABOVE: A Royal Army Ordnance Corps air transportable boot repair
trailer, c1950. BELOW: A Royal Army Ordnance Corps mobile laundry
washing machine, c1950.

days before the outbreak of war. The Mount Pleasant Sorting Office swung into action, initially with a 'key party' and then with reservists and volunteers, but it was not long before safety considerations (the threat of bombing) brought a move to Reading, then later to Bournemouth and Nottingham; equally it was not long before history repeated itself on the question of unit locations, or rather lack of information on them.

Probably the most important postal innovation of the war was the airgraph, a Kodak idea, which led to the Air Letter. Its introduction in May 1941 led to a notable improvement in mail from the Middle East, using as it did minimal space in aircraft. Microfilms of letters and addresses written on special forms were photographed and rolls of negatives were sent to UK by air. In UK positive prints of the films were made, smaller than the original forms; these were then posted free in windowed envelopes, through normal postal channels.

Postal arrangements in North Africa were perhaps typical: at the end of the campaign in 1943 there were fifty-three British Army Post Offices serving the Lines of Communication areas and thirty-six British Forces Post Offices with operational formations. The Base Army Post Office in Cairo was the centre of this organisation. The war in the Western Desert, especially the long forward movements, but not forgetting the retreats caused by Rommel's successes, provided a searching test of the army Postal Service. In the fluid battles, when even Corps and Divisional HQs were over-run by German forces, postal units had their moments of excitement and share of casualties.

For the attack on Europe a new 'closed address' system was introduced – this would not only obviate security problems at a time when the point of landing was a closely guarded secret but also be easier to handle. This system worked perfectly and the Oxford Street organisation moved to France on D+10, thus making it possible to give a

continuous service to troops when they moved to France.

As the Allies moved through France, Belgium and Holland postal roadheads moved forward as quickly as they could. Eventually the Allies moved into Germany and airfields were brought into use as they were captured, thus allowing the mail service to achieve the highest standards in supporting the army. Then it was demobilization again, a difficult time when the assistance of German and Belgian civilians was appreciated. Fortunately the army appeared to have learnt from past mistakes – there was no question of the Postal Service becoming a Reserve Force again.

The Royal Army Ordnance Corps played a major and essential part in the Second World War. Starting with a nucleus of a few hundred officers and a few thousand men of the Regular and Territorial Army, the Corps developed in little more than four years into an efficient organisation of 8,000 officers and 130,000 men.

From the Ordnance Directorate in the War Office, which dealt with policy, Corps organisation world-wide and the provision of stores, vehicles and ammunition, a UK base was created to supply all items of Ordnance concern to all theatres; this was complemented by a smaller base in the Middle East and a comprehensive Field Force organization which provided a reliable and flexible system for the maintenance of a Field Army. This consisted of Ordnance Field Parks, Forward Maintenance Ammunition Sections, Forward Maintenance Stores Sections, Mobile Laundry and Bath Units, Mobile Ammunition Repair Units, Ordnance Beach Detachments and Industrial Gas Units. Base and Lines of Communication units in theatres of operations were Base Ordnance Depots, Base Ammunition Depots, Vehicle Depots, Base and Hospital Laundries, Base Industrial Gas Units, Port Ordnance and Ammunition Detachments. The war saw the creation of a large workshop organization for the repair, recovery and manufacture of a large range of equipment at the base and in

ABOVE: Royal Pioneer Corps trainees on road maintenance. LEFT: Sharpening bayonets; RIGHT: DUKWs of 20 Maritime Regiment Royal Corps of Transport exercising in Jersey, 1972.

the field, which was transferred on the creation of the Royal Electrical and Mechanical Engineers in 1942.

Within this variety of services the changing face of warfare demanded considerable flexibility. The UK depot organisation became, in some cases unwillingly, the largest employers of the new Auxiliary Territorial Service (ATS), introducing the girls to a variety of tasks employing the latest techniques in mechanical handling and card–based information technology. In the field, units which had previously come to rely on static locations had to develop new techniques and equipment to become mobile. As the war spread throughout the world, the Royal Army Ordnance Corps became world leaders in the packing of stores to protect them from the ravages of varied climates.

Ordnance success in the war can be said to be based on the integration of staffs and commands at all levels, which had never been achieved before, as well as a close and direct control from Whitehall, tackling the acute shortages early in the war, and complicated and ambitious projects later. The Corps supplied fighting troops with ever-increasing amounts of arms, equipment and ammunition. Success did not come easily but it resulted from major effort and dedicated work throughout the world.

As in the Great War of 1914-18 the Royal Army Service Corps expanded greatly during the Second World War to meet the wide range of activities which came its way. 10,000 strong in 1939, it rose to 325,000 men in 1945 – one soldier in every ten wore the Royal Army Service Corps badge – and the Corps' achievements relate to its numbers.

As with its sister Corps, the Royal Army Service Corps was directed from a number of Supply and Transport Branches in the War Office. The Corps was fortunate in the quality and experience of its officers, and provided the first head of REME on its formation in 1942, Major General Bertram Rowcroft. Wherever the army served there were to be found units of the Royal Army Service Corps and, with its Staff Clerks in most embassies

throughout the world, the Corps was also represented where there were no other units.

While the 3-ton truck was the main work-horse of the Corps in all theatres, the war saw a number of interesting developments in other forms of transport and supply. For the Norway expedition in 1940, for example, the composite ration was introduced, and then developed over the next few years so that soldiers had a choice of menu. When German stocks of petrol were captured in North Africa in 1940 the German container was found to be far superior to the old British 'flimsie' and the 'jerrican' immediately replaced it.

Pack transport was used in difficult terrain, in France in 1940 by the Royal Indian Army Service Corps, and later in North Africa, Sicily and Italy. Tank transporters came into their own on long hauls along the North African coastline, the Diamond Ts having been delivered direct from America to the 1st Army; their use in Italy and North-West Europe confirmed their place in the order of battle for post-war use.

Although two occasions are recorded in the Great War when supplies or ammunition were dropped from aircraft (Kut-el-Almara and Arras), air despatch was first used extensively in Burma, again led by the Royal Indian Army Service Corps, in order to resupply our troops fighting the Japanese; this provided a close link with the Royal Air Force which has continued ever since. Efforts by air despatchers to supply surrounded airborne troops at Arnhem led to heavy casualties and a reputation second to none for determination and gallantry.

The amphibious DUKWs, too, earned their place in history in Italy 1943-44 and in North-West Europe; less well-known but equally deserving was their use in Burma, largely on the River Irrawaddy, including being used as assault craft, a role equalled by the Fantails of the Armoured Amphibious Regiment in infantry actions on Lake Comacchio in Italy in 1944. Not be forgotten is the extensive use of water transport, generally in British waters but also in the Mediterranean, particularly in Malta when every vessel was hit by enemy

ABOVE: Royal Army Service Corps MT training at Blackdown, 1945.
BELOW: A Royal Corps of Transport troop in Bulford, 1980s.

fire. Tales of bravery abound, from the last boat to leave the beaches of Dunkirk in 1940, the RASC vessel *Marlborough*, which left under tow, both her propellers having been blown off, to mine–dodging (invariably) off Normandy, and life-saving from a part of the Mulberry Harbour breaking up in a great storm. Life in the Royal Army Service Corps Fleet, a function which had been taken over in 1891 as the War Department Fleet, was never dull.

On the Burma border in January 1944 an Ordnance Divisional Sub-park, acting as infantry, held off a series of heavy Japanese attacks for seventeen days while issuing stores to surrounding units under extremely difficult circumstances. In fact, while life in a logistic Corps is not often as exciting as it is from time to time in a Teeth Arm unit, and the routine duties rarely attract media cover, logistic troops have always worked consistently hard throughout the course of any campaign. Infantry units might withdraw for rest and recuperation, but no logistic units have ever enjoyed that comparative luxury.

The end of the Second World War in 1945 should have brought peace, but occupation duties and other world-wide commitments in the final years of the Empire saw British forces extensively involved in brush– fire wars. The following involvements are not exhaustive but they do give an idea of life in the army, indeed in all Corps forming The Royal Logistic Corps: Palestine 1945-48, Malaya 1948-60, Kenya (Mau Mau) 1952-56, Korea 1950-56, Aden 1958-67, Cyprus (Eoka terrorists) 1955-60, Suez 1956, Brunei, Borneo and Sarawak 1962-66, Falklands 1982, The Gulf 1991-1992, Yugoslavia 1992 to date, not forgetting the Northern Ireland problem since 1969.

A world war may have come to an end but development within the army continued, in the search to improve, and inevitably to do more with less. The Postal Services became involved with NATO headquarters in the early 1950s and from 1953 gradually took on the transmission of classified mails world-

wide. In 1962 the Home Postal Depot moved from Acton to Mill Hill, London, its present location and, having previously accepted responsibility for RAF mails, took over HM Ships' mail from the Post Office, thus becoming both a Tri-Service and an international military service. Further developments and changes of name have taken place since then and in July 1992 the Minister of State for the Armed Forces launched the Defence Postal and Courier Services Defence Support Agency at Mill Hill. This status allowed the Royal Engineers Postal & Courier Service in the UK to operate along more commercial lines, streamline its operation and expand its entreprenurial activities within a specified budget from the government.

In 1945, having reached a strength of 70,000 during the war, the Army Catering Corps remained in the Order of Battle and was therefore able to continue the improvements initiated by Sir Isidore Salmon. The key was the introduction of apprenticeships, started in 1947, which led to the creation of a Corps of top–class tradesmen who can hold their own anywhere in the world of catering. From simple beginnings in 1937-38 with regimental cooks at Hotelympia to the present day, chefs have been outstandingly successful and the Corps has built a reputation for being one of the leading organizations in the UK catering area. Prime Minister's Conferences, Commonwealth leaders' meetings, Chequers weekends and a number of Embassy functions have all involved Army Catering Corps chefs. They have scaled the highest levels in their profession, and all units throughout the British Army have benefitted from their expertise.

In 1946 the Pioneer Corps was granted the title 'Royal' in recognition of its meritorious work during the years 1939–45. Like all other Corps, however, it was much reduced in size after the war, while still retaining extensive commitments. Unlike after the Great War, the Corps was retained as part of the permanent post-war Regular Army, and was honoured in

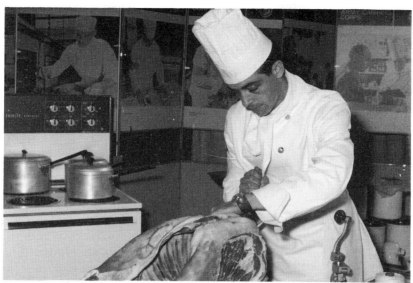

ABOVE: Butchery instruction in the Army School of Catering, Aldershot. BELOW: Commemoration stone marking the 50th anniversary of the Army Catering Corps, 22 March 1991, Queen's Avenue, Aldershot.

33

June 1977 by the appointment of HRH the Duke of Gloucester as Colonel-in-Chief. The Corps HQ occupied several locations during the Second World War, and their travels ceased only in September 1960 when they occupied Quebec Barracks, Northampton (renamed Simpson Barracks in 1961), having got to know Stourport in 1947 and Wrexham in 1949. The happy links with Northampton are retained.

It was in 1948 that the Royal Army Ordnance Corps moved from Leicester to Deepcut – its headquarters had moved several times during the war, so it was reassuring to settle in such a pleasant area, especially since this move allowed the concentration of the HQ Training Centre, the Depot & Training Battalion, the School of Ordnance and the Apprentices College. The Corps' position in the army was greatly enhanced by its tremendous contribution to the war effort; at last commanders and staffs in the War Office and elsewhere seemed to have learnt from history and Royal Army Ordnance Corps officers and men took their place as respected equals in the army.

Having lost responsibility for ammunition after the Great War to the civilian Chief Inspector of Armaments, the Corps regained the task in 1939, and after the Second World War extensive changes took place. Hand in hand with the School of Ammunition, the story of the Royal Army Ordnance Corps ammunition organisation is one of continued and progressive success.

Explosive Ordnance Disposal is an area of activity seen and appreciated by the army and general public alike. Involvement in Cyprus, Aden and Hong Kong in the 1950s led to major effort in Northern Ireland. Close liaison with the Royal Ulster Constabulary and units on the ground, coupled with the introduction of sophisticated equipment, notably the 'Wheelbarrow', has resulted in frequent frustration for the Irish Republican Army and the saving of many lives and much property. Recognition of this gallant work is shown in the award of six George Crosses and sixty-eight George Medals since 1940.

The recommendations of the McLeod Committee saw a number of changes take place in 1965 which affected several Corps, a step in some ways towards the creation of The Royal Logistic Corps in 1993. The three great QMG Services, Royal Army Service Corps, Royal Army Ordnance Corps and Royal Electrical & Mechanical Engineers, duplicated each other in many ways, particularly as regards provisioning, stores holding and transport management and control. It was decided that the Royal Army Service Corps should become the transport and distribution Corps of the army, taking over from the Royal Engineers railways, port operations and movement control, each function having its own distinguished history with the Royal Engineers; it should transfer responsibility for supply and fuel provisioning and stores holding, the Fire Service, Barrack Services and Staff Clerks to the Royal Army Ordnance Corps. Meanwhile the Royal Army Ordnance Corps took over the provision of Royal Engineers plant and machinery. Whereas the Royal Army Service Corps had its name changed to the Royal Corps of Transport, its ninth change in two hundred years, the Royal Army Ordnance Corps, as the army's provisioning and stores holding Corps, escaped the implementation of General McLeod's recommendation that it should be renamed the Supply Corps, to everyone's relief.

In 1951 the Royal Army Service Corps lost its remaining unit workshops to the Royal Electrical & Mechanical Engineers, and in 1957 its armoured transport regiment role to the Royal Armoured Corps, although the Royal Corps of Transport has effectively taken on the latter role in Northern Ireland with great efficiency. Post-war losses continued with the Bridging Regiment in 1970 when M2 bridges were introduced, the Longmoor Railway in 1969, the last horse transport company in UK in 1970 and in Hong Kong in 1976, aircraft liaison flights in 1970, the hovercraft squadron in 1974, along with that well-loved but thirty-two year old amphibian, the DUKW. Old friends inevitably go, but

LEFT: Silver globe commissioned by the Royal Pioneer Corps in 1967; RIGHT: 1879 silver stag presented to the Army Catering Corps by the Worshipful Company of Cooks in 1976. BELOW: The Royal Waggon Train in the Peninsula 1812, commissioned by the Royal Corps of Transport to celebrate two centuries of support to the British Army.

progressive efficiency and operational involvements of the Corps 'as well as its high *esprit de corps*, particularly noticeable since 1965, more than made up for this.

While the air despatch organisation has been reduced, so that now only one Regular Squadron and a Territorial Army troop keep these skills alive, assistance throughout the world continued: Zimbabwe, Nepal, Ethiopia and Iraq are but four well-publicized examples.

HRH the Duke of Gloucester, Colonel-in-Chief of the Royal Corps of Transport, died in June 1974, having several years earlier laid the foundation stone of the 'new' Buller Barracks in Aldershot; in February 1975 HRH Princess Alice, Duchess of Gloucester, was appointed the Corps' new, and last, Colonel-in-Chief. HM The Queen became Colonel-in-Chief of the Royal Army Ordnance Corps in 1953, replacing her father, HM King George VI who, as Duke of York, accepted the position in 1922 and remained Colonel-in-Chief until his death.

These pages on predecessors of The Royal Logistic Corps are intended to give an outline of how logistic support for the army has developed over two hundred years and more. It is impossible to do full justice to every Corps and much information has quickly been explained or simply summarised.

What is evident, however, is that The Royal Logistic Corps starts life as a multi-skilled community, a large and hugely gifted team, whose predecessors served under a variety of different capbadges in every part of the world where the army has been stationed. The traditions and achievements of the past are an inspiration for the logistic soldier of today and a solid base in an ever-changing world.

## The Princess Royal Barracks

**Location:** The Princess Royal Barracks, part of which stand on top of Chobham Ridges, are based around the small village of Deepcut, which derives its name from the cutting dug out to carry the neighbouring Basingstoke Canal.

**Early Days:** During the end of the 18th and early part of the 19th century the surrounding local area had been used by the British Army for training purposes. It was ideal, in that it enabled large concentrations of troops to exercise together. A number of temporary encampments were set up, of which the most significant probably was the one held during the summer of 1853 on Chobham Common just prior to the outbreak of the Crimean War in 1854. It was this camp which led to a proposal for a permanent training camp in the area.

Aldershot Heath was selected and purchased in 1854. At first only a summer tented camp was envisaged, but the needs of the Crimean War led to the building of a military camp in 1855 at Aldershot. The camp expanded rapidly and Aldershot became the only complete military town built in the United Kingdom since the Roman occupation; however, by the end of the 19th century, there was a need for additional barracks. It was during the Boer War of 1899-1902 that a decision was taken by the War Department to concentrate three Regular Divisions at Aldershot as part of the 1st Army Corps which led to the building of a number of new camps nearby, at Bulford, Deepcut, Longmoor and Tidworth.

**The Building of the Camp:** The land on which the barracks were built was purchased by the War Department in the 1890s: 252 acres, acquired for £20,250.

The Royal Engineers started building in 1900. The positions of the barracks as we know them today were different, as the south end of Blackdown Camp was known as Deepcut and the northern end was known as Blackdown. Deepcut Barracks were built to house two brigades of field artillery (known later as Artillery Lines), while Blackdown Barracks housed two infantry battalions.

The actual barrack buildings were a mixture of corrugated iron and wooden huts, and brick buildings. They were named after battles similar to the barracks forming part of Aldershot Camp. Blackdown Barracks

ABOVE: The Royal Army Ordnance Corps in Ajax Bay during the Falklands War 1982. Painting by Joan Wanklyn. BELOW: Pioneers on Sword Beach, Normandy on D-Day 1944. This Terence Cuneo painting was commissioned by the Royal Pioneer Corps on its amalgamation in The Royal Logistic Corps.

consisted of Dettingen, a battle fought in June 1743 during the War of the Austrian Succession, and Alma, a battle fought in September 1854 during the Crimean War. Deepcut Barracks consisted of North and South Minden, Minden being a battle fought in August 1759 during the Seven Years War.

The barracks were completed by early 1903 and were first occupied by 18 and 20 Brigades of the Royal Field Artillery (Deepcut), followed by 1st Battalion Royal Scots and 2nd Battalion The King's Own (Royal Lancaster Regiment) (Blackdown), the latter two having just returned from the Boer War. Thereafter they were occupied by a succession of artillery and infantry regiments, many of which have now been either amalgamated or disbanded.

**The First World War:** It was the outbreak of the First World War in 1914 which brought about further developments. The Bisley Railway was extended in 1915 in order to transport the thousands of troops who were to pass through and, with the advent of air warfare and anti-aircraft operations, Frith Barracks (Blackdown) were built on Frith Hill to house an anti-aircraft brigade of three batteries of Royal Artillery, a search-light battalion of Royal Engineers and a Signals Company. Two further barracks were built at Blackdown – Aisne and Marne, battles fought in 1914.

**The Inter-War and Second World War Years:** After the First World War the barracks returned to normality, but they were soon to become the home of the 6th Infantry Brigade, part of Aldershot Command. This was an experimental formation in which ideas on organisation, mechanisation, weapons and tactics were tried out. The brigade consisted of four battalions of infantry and support units which were changed every few years. Regiments stationed there during these years as part of the brigade were: the South Wales Borderers, Sherwood Foresters, Devonshires, Northamptonshires, King's Own Yorkshire Light Infantry, Suffolks, Somerset Light Infantry, Durham Light Infantry, Devon and Cornwall Light Infantry, Royal Berkshires and Royal Welsh Fusiliers. 9 Company Royal Army Services Corps (Horse Transport) was stationed in the barracks in 1920-21 before it converted to mechanical transport and moved to Constantinople. Before long Britain was plunged into the Second World War and in 1939 this area became the home for many thousands of troops, British and Canadian.

**Post 1945:** When the war ended in 1945 the barracks were run down, apart from a period when they were used as a Royal Artillery Officer Cadet Training Unit, until June 1948, when the Headquarters and No 4 Training Battalion Royal Army Ordnance Corps first moved into Minden Barracks, Deepcut (Blackdown) from Tidworth. In 1949 No 4 Trade Training Battalion moved into Blackdown, later to be followed by other Royal Army Ordnance Corps units. By 1962 Blackdown had become the Regimental Depot & Training Centre of the Royal Army Ordnance Corps

By the mid-1960s the old barracks had become outdated and plans were put forward to rebuild them. Between 1967 and 1971 the old Minden Barracks, Deepcut, were demolished and replaced with a modern barracks, renamed Blackdown Barracks. The new Headquarters and Training Centre was opened by Her Majesty The Queen in May 1972.

Since the 1960s several of the original barracks have disappeared, but some still remain, such as Dettingen and Alma, now empty. One can still see parts of South Minden Barracks, which 37 Squadron Royal Corps of Transport occupied from July 1965 until the unit became a detachment of 41 Squadron based in Aldershot.

In summary, the camp has a history going back to 1900 and has been occupied at different times by a variety of regiments and Corps. Royal Army Service Corps occupation

ABOVE: Royal Corps of Transport silver centrepiece commissioned to commemorate two centuries of support to the British Army. BELOW: First air post operated by the Royal Engineers and Royal Air Force between Folkestone and Cologne in 1919. Painting by Terence Cuneo.

was first recorded in 1920, and the Royal Army Ordnance Corps have been major occupiers since 1948, with the Royal Corps of Transport returning in 1965. They were the largest components of The Royal Logistic Corps, whose home the barracks have now become. Another page in history turns.

**The Old Railway Line:** There was once a railway line between Brookwood and Blackdown Camp. Opened in 1890, and known as the Bisley Branch Line, it originally ran from Brookwood to Bisley Camp and was used once a year for the annual rifle shooting competition. The two–coach train used was nicknamed 'The Bisley Bullet'.

The First World War and the building of new camps at Pirbright, Deepcut and Blackdown meant a need to transport thousands of troops.

This resulted in the extension of the railway into the new camps, and it was the Royal Engineers and German prisoners-of-war (the latter were in a fenced off camp at nearby Frith Hill) who did most of the work. The three mile branch was opened by Their Majesties King George V and Queen Mary, who travelled along the line to visit the troops. The railway line to Blackdown Camp, however, had only a short life, for it was discontinued in 1921, although the line to Bisley Camp was used until 1952, when it too was closed. There are still signs today of the overgrown old track.

### St Barbara's Garrison Church

The Garrison Church, now known as St Barbara's, was built at Deepcut in 1901 to serve the units stationed in the area. The records show that the first service to be held in the new church took place on 31 March 1901. In 1905 one acre of land adjoining the church was acquired from the Crown and a burial ground was consecrated by the Chaplain General.

The early history of the church is sketchy. Regular services were held but attendance was never high, the common excuse being the state of the weather. Near the church was the Soldiers Home (now demolished) where meetings of the Church of England Men's Society, the Guild of St Helena and bible classes were held. On Sunday evenings lantern slide services were held, which always guaranteed a good turn-out.

Originally the church was lit by candles and did not have an electric light until 1911. The first marriage ceremony under the Marriage (Naval, Military and Air Force) Act of 1932 was conducted at the church on 31 March 1934.

On 1 October 1967 the church was renamed St Barbara's Garrison Church, and much of the property of St Barbara's Church, Hilsea was moved to Deepcut, including the pipe organ, pulpit and the 1914-1919 Royal Army Ordnance Corps Roll of Honour. Several other Corps memorials were transferred from Hilsea.

Today St Barbara's Garrison Church is used by both military and the civilian residents of the village of Deepcut. The Corps presence was acknowledged on Corps Sunday 1993 with the dedication of a brass plate showing the establishment of The Royal Logistic Corps from the Forming Corps. On Corps Sunday 1994 a commemorative RLC window was unveiled, featuring the Formation Parade in April 1993. The Royal Logistic Corps Book of Remembrance has been placed in the church.

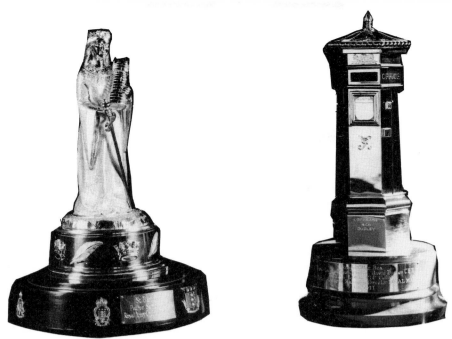

LEFT: St Barbara, patron saint of the Royal Army Ordnance Corps; RIGHT: Silver post box presented to The Royal Logistic Corps by the Post Office in 1993. BELOW: 'Sustaining Forward' by Terence Cuneo. The Army Catering Corps feeding elements of 7th Armoured Brigade during the 1991 Gulf War.

# FORMATION

## The Logistic Support Review
### Major General A N Carlier OBE

Many reading this book will not know the background to the Logistic Support Review (LSR) which had its genesis in 1989. At that time there was a wide-spread view that the logistic support to the army could be provided more efficiently and economically. This view was felt keenly at the junior working level of the logistic Corps and it was here that any change would be more readily acceptable. Those who had served most of their career in 'the system' viewed any change to accepted practices with grave concern, scepticism and even abhorrence. Many industrial concerns inject change as a way of freshening a system and, although this was not the compelling reason for change within the army, undoubtedly a review of the whole way the army did its logistic business was overdue and would probably prove to be of considerable benefit. Many, however, did not agree with this view and the LSR team knew they would need to have compelling arguments if any of their thoughts were to gain any form of acceptability as future practice.

The LSR team was given terms of reference with these objectives: To examine the army's logistic support organisation and systems, to establish how the task of providing logistic support for the Army in peace, transition to war, and war might be performed most efficiently, effectively and economically, and to make recommendations.

This was a broad aim and the introduction of the word 'economically' was significant at the time when manpower and cash savings were needed in the army as a whole. The study team was also to review command and control, the logistic support to the Field Army, and to determine if savings could be made by rationalisation and amalgamation within the existing system. The scope for increased civilianisation was also to be considered as this was seen to be a cheaper option than the use of military manpower.

The very words of the aim and the additional factors to be considered sent shudders down the spines of the older generation. Many retired officers saw danger in this review and made their views known from an early date, applying pressure on those in influential positions. In spite of this the team found a genuine desire by many in the logistic Corps for change and especially for rationalisation. At times, the team members had to set aside pangs of personal concern as they could see the effect the study would have on their own Corps. It is much to their credit that they survived some criticism of a lack of loyalty as the likely pattern for the future evolved.

The team endeavoured to retain functions where possible and proposed a linking of these where they were complimentary. We held firmly to the view that, if any element of the logistic support to the army was left out of the future structure, then predators would soon sweep down in the relentless aim to find savings to keep the 'front line first' to the detriment of the logistic system as a whole. The team felt that it would be better for all concerned to link the smaller element of the logistic system with their bigger brothers and thus afford to them a degree of protection while at the same time retaining their important logistic functions.

The result is now well known and few changes were made to the recommendations of the team when the time came to implement the new system. The logistic Corps are a powerful voice in the army today and possibly are better respected and acknowledged now than before the changes. The achievements in the Gulf, in Bosnia and in Rwanda have generated a greater faith in the system, an increased acknowledgement the professionalism involved and an understanding of the need for an efficient and economic system that will work well when tested in adverse conditions. The successes so far are attributable to many people but special mention must be made to those at the working level. No system, however carefully designed, will be perfect and reliance on the enthusiasm of the junior commander was always considered to be a major factor in the success of the LSR.

ABOVE: Director Generals and Directors of the Forming Corps
re-badging parties at the start of the Formation Parade in Deepcut.
BELOW: Inspection by the Colonel-in-Chief during the Formation
Parade in Deepcut.

The question has been posed, 'Would the Team have done anything different?' Had we had the time we would have trialed some of the ideas we put forward. No doubt some minor adjustments would have been made. However, the basic principles would not have changed in the light of experience. There was a clear need for change and rationalisation was high on the agenda. We might have tried harder to remove emotion from the debate but this would probably have proved not possible where change was resisted. We wondered if we had generated too large a Royal Logistic Corps and if it was too big to manage. We were concerned that the task of command and control of the Corps might have been too great for one organisation but, on balance, we felt that there was no better way of achieving our aims. We might have injected a little more senior staff support into QMG's area, but such a move would have been unacceptable in the army as a whole under pressure to reduce the rank structure wherever possible. In hindsight, we might have strengthened our arguments on this point but this was left for others to do in the light of experience. It is unlikely we would have made any change to the establishment of the Director General Equipment Support as the team felt it important that those repairing equipment should have control over the spare parts needed.

The logistic systems proposed by the LSR are now well established under the new structure. Manpower savings have been made, there has been considerable financial benefit and the new Corps is certainly earning its spurs in the eyes of the rest of the army. Those who saw the logistic side of army life as a drain on resources that could be used elsewhere have been made to sit up and take note. This is a credit to all logisticians, be they ex-RE, RCT, RAOC, RPC or ACC and also civilian!

**Logistic Support Review.** In 1989, the then Quartermaster General instituted the wide ranging Logistic Support Review (LSR). The aim of the study was to recommend the most efficient organisations to support the Army.

There was a political and budgetary imperative to achieve a reduction in the so called 'teeth to tail' ratio. Shortly after the study team began its work the strategic environment, within which the British Army had been operating for the past forty-five years, changed suddenly and profoundly with the collapse of the Iron Curtain. Inevitably, there was an immediate pressure to produce a 'peace dividend' and in July 1991 the Government announced its proposals for Britain's future defence, known as 'Options for Change'. For the army this meant reducing its trained strength to 104,000 by 1 April 1995 and also withdrawing large numbers of troops and equipment from Germany to the United Kingdom.

The LSR team's report, issued in June 1991, recommended that the future structure of logistics in the British Army should be organised on a three pillar system:

**The Three Pillars**
Logistic Support
Staff
Equipment Support
The Central Pillar, the G4 Staff, was to be responsible for logistic policy, planning and central resource management; the two functional pillars, Logistic Support and Equipment Support, were to be responsible respectively for support to the soldier and supporting the army's equipment. This structure was to be established at the Ministry of Defence in Headquarters Quartermaster General, and mirrored in all headquarters down to brigade level. All those functions undertaken by the Royal Corps of Transport, Royal Army Ordnance Corps, Royal Pioner Corps, Army Catering Corps and the Postal and Courier elements of the Royal Engineers would in future be the responsibility of one new Corps, The Royal Logistic Corps. The REME would take over responsibility for the equipment and supply management of motor transport and technical stores and vehicles from the Royal Army Ordnance Corps.

These recommendations meant the demise of four separate and independent Corps, and, as *esprit de corps*, inherent in the British regimental system, has always been a major

44

ABOVE: Inspection of the Staff band on the Formation Parade in Deepcut. On the right are Captain S J Smith, HRH, the Drum Major, Captain R E W Maycock and the Representative Colonel Commandant, Major General C E G Carrington. BELOW: March Past of the Hong Kong Formation Day Parade led by Major C J Griggs (Hong Kong Logistic Support Regiment).

influence, amalgamations on the scale proposed made for a radical move.

The operational task of setting up establishments, equipment tables, the drawdown of the British Army of the Rhine and creating coordinated centres of training was managed through the existing policy branches of the Forming Corps. These plans ran concurrently with those to manage the reduction of 35% of manpower required under Options for Change.

**Regimental Matters.** The establishment of the Regimental Headquarters was agreed in September 1992 but only a small team of four officers and six clerical staff was available to plan the transition into a single Corps by 5 April 1993. The key events were twofold: firstly the establishment of a Trust Fund, a Regimental Association and the management of the One Day's Pay Scheme, and secondly the establishment of dress regulations and managing the production and availability of all items of dress and accoutrements in time for formation parades throughout the Army. The new Corps, established to supply the army, had to be able to supply itself. The extracts below illustrate the breadth of activities dealt with in the early period.

**Visit of the Private Secretary to The Princess Royal – 21 October 1992**

1. *General.* I was received with great warmth and appreciation. He had seen the Cameron letter about Royal Military Police/Adjutant General's Corps in the paper and wanted to know if we had any such problems. I reassured him.

2. *Photographs.* I had earlier confirmed that no Royal photographs are provided at public expense. There is a system for applying for signed photographs of The Queen and Prince Philip, but it is only a control mechanism to save the Royal hand! Private Secretary noted his irritation with the photographer copyright system and said that it affects all organisations. He said that the Wrens had tried to get around it by arranging for a Naval photographer. I said that we would not wish to repeat the Wren's experiment and asked if we could use a recommended photographer. I reminded Private Secretary that we had three Royal Colonels and suggested that we could find an honorarium by way of a sitting payment. I also mentioned that we would want the ladies to wear regimental brooches and the Duke to wear uniform. He thought this was a splendid idea and will get back to me.

*A letter from the Regimental Colonel to the Director General          October 1992.*

**Buckingham Palace** 6 November 1992 Thank you for your letter concerning the re-naming of barracks.

The Princess Royal has agreed to the use of her name for the barracks at Blackdown and Gutersloh.

*A letter to the Regimental Colonel*

**Her Royal Highness The Princess Royal** Buckingham Palace

The future Colonels Commandant of The Royal Logistic Corps and Director General, Logistic Support (Army) and his Staff send loyal greetings and best wishes on your forthcoming marriage.
*Regimental Headquarters*
*The Royal Logistic Corps.          10 December 1992*

**The Famous Five.** In the fifteen months before The RLC was formed, the Directors General and Directors of the five forming Corps were having regular meetings to discuss the host of problems which arose from the significant task of amalgamation and adoption of the Logistic Support Review. The then Quartermaster General, General Sir John Learmont, nicknamed this key group 'The Famous Five', a term which stuck, so that all meetings became 'Famous Five Meetings' and the abbreviation in Andover for the esteemed body became, simply, The FF.

# ON PARADE
## QUICK MARCH

Solo B♭ Cornet

ALBERT ELMS

ABOVE: 'The Famous Five': (clockwise from near left to right) Brigadier M A Browne, Major General J D MacDonald CB CBE, Colonel C M Lake (Regimental Colonel), Major General D L Burden CBE, Major General D F E Botting CB CBE, Brigadier C B Telfer CBE ADC, Brigadier A B Atkinson CBE. BELOW: The score of the Corps March 'On Parade'.

The first time this phrase was coined, I immediately scanned the shelves of my children's bedrooms to find suitable book covers, which were then transferred onto slides for the many presentations on LSR matters which we had to give at the time. *Five Get Into a Fix* was a (popular one in the early days, followed by *Five Get Into Trouble* and *The Famous Five and the Strange Legacy*. When the Dress Committee was deciding on our new uniforms *The Famous Five in Fancy Dress* was a popular title and eventually in April 1993 we had *Five Run Away Together*. One slide which was produced but which never seemed to be used was *Five Have Plenty of Fun.*
*Lieutenant Colonel J R Wallace OBE, 4 General Support Regiment*

## Regimental Cypher

We spoke last week about a Regimental Cypher for The Royal Logistic Corps.

You will be aware that each of the Forming Corps (Royal Corps of Transport, Royal Army Ordnance Corps, Postal and Courier Services (Royal Engineers), Royal Pioneer Corps and Army Catering Corps) enjoys the privilege of a Cypher; in each case a Monarchal Crown above the initial letters of the Corps title.

I attach a representation of the proposed Cypher and I would be grateful if you could arrange for it to be copied for submission to Her Majesty.

I regret that there is a time imperative, because we hope to have items of mess property marked with the Cypher in time for our formation on 5 April 1993. I would be grateful, therefore, if you could agree to giving the matter some priority
*A letter to the College of Arms*
*from the Regimental Colonel*

## Formation Parade – Press Release
### BUCKINGHAM PALACE
### HRH The Princess Royal's Office

Monday 5 April 1993
The Princess Royal, Colonel-in-Chief, The Royal Logistic Corps, will take the salute at the Inauguration Parade for The Royal Logistic Corps, Blackdown Barracks, Deepcut, Camberley, Surrey.
**(To be released to the Press on 14 December)**

## Regimental Alliances and Affiliation
### Alliances
### Australia
Royal Australian Corps of Transport
Royal Australian Army Ordnance Corps
Australian Army Catering Corps
### New Zealand
Royal New Zealand Corps of Transport
Royal New Zealand Army Ordnance Corps
### India
Army Service Corps of India
Army Ordnance Corps of India
### Pakistan
Army Service Corps of Pakistan
Army Ordnance Corps of Pakistan
### Sri Lanka
The Sri Lankan Army Service Corps
The Sri Lankan Army Ordnance Corps
### Malaysia
The Malaysian Army Service Corps
The Malaysian Army Ordnance Corps
### Affiliation
Queen's Own Gurkha Transport Regiment
### Livery Companies of London
An association has been established between The Royal Logistic Corps and the following Livery Companies:
The Worshipful Company of Cooks
The Worshipful Company of Gold and Silver Wyre Drawers
The Worshipful Company of Carmen

## Formation Day in Deepcut
The Royal Logistic Corps was born on a day of rain, wind and sunshine. Monday 5 April 1993 was marked by parades in various parts of the United Kingdom and abroad, but the central Formation Day parade was held in Deepcut, attended by the Colonel-in-Chief, HRH The Princess Royal. Also present were the Representative Colonel Commandant, Major General C E G Carrington CB CBE, the Director General Logistic Support (Army), Major General D L Burden CBE, the Colonels Commandant of the Royal Logistic Corps as

ABOVE: The Colonels Commandant with the Colonel-in-Chief on Formation Day. BELOW: The Colonel-in-Chief, Representative Colonel Commandant and the Director General Logistic Support (Army) at a Luncheon for Commanding Officers of the Corps, 1993.

well as Directors of the Forming Corps, Major General J D MacDonald CB CBE, Director General Transport and Movements, Major General D F E Botting, CB CBE, Director General Ordnance Services, Brigadier M A Browne, Chief Executive Postal & Courier Service, Brigadier C B Telfer CBE ADC, Director Army Pioneers & Labour, and Brigadier A B Atkinson CBE, Director Army Catering Corps.

The Princess Royal arrived by helicopter and was greeted by the Representative Colonel Commandant and the Regimental Colonel, Colonel C M Lake. At the Headquarters RLC Officers' Mess she was greeted by the President of the Mess Committee, Major A Ward, before she signed the Visitors' Book. She then drove to the parade ground where some 500 men were on parade, commanded by Lieutenant Colonel R Elliott, accompanied by the Staff Band of The Royal Logistic Corps, directed by Captain R E W Maycock and Captain S J Smith. 800 spectators braved the horizontal rain which somehow seemed to ignore the awnings covering the stands. Radio and television covered the event and national and local papers published articles, as did *Soldier* magazine. The monsoon-like weather miraculously stopped shortly before the parade marched on, giving way to bright sunlight. Somehow it seemed to augur well for the new Corps.

After the parade presented arms to the Colonel-in-Chief an act of symbolism initiated the parade. Representative officers, NCOs and men of the Royal Engineers, Royal Corps of Transport, Royal Army Ordnance Corps, Royal Pioneer Corps and the Army Catering Corps marched on to the centre of the parade. Heads of the Forming Corps then marched on and presented new head-dress and the new Corps badge to their respective Corps soldiers. The Forming Corps flags were lowered and the Royal Logistic Corps flag was raised. The old Corps were seen to be no more.

Accompanied by the representative Colonel Commandant and the Parade Commander, the Princess Royal inspected the parade, speaking to many of the men and women taking part, both Regular and Territorial Army. After the Advance in Review Order, HRH addressed the parade. 'The Royal Logistic Corps has a vital role', she said. 'You have all worked very efficiently in the past in your own units, often unnoticed. I realize the amalgamation will have caused regret among retired and serving members of the old Corps but I am sure that The Royal Logistic Corps' reputation will be a source of pride, and you can look forward to the future with confidence'. The Staff Band of The Royal Logistic Corps brought up the rear of the parade as it marched off to the Corps March, *On Parade*.

On her way to the Corps Museum, the Princess Royal planted a commemorative walnut tree adjacent to the Royal Way, which had been opened by HM The Queen only days before, and unveiled a plaque renaming the barracks 'The Princess Royal Barracks Blackdown'. After the lengthy tour of the museum, guided by the Curator, Lieutenant Colonel (Retired) W P Masterson, HRH attended a Reception and Luncheon in The Royal Logistic Corps Training Centre Sergeants' mess where, after having been met by the PMC, Warrant Officer One (Staff Sergeant Major) Parkin BEM, she met a number of serving and retired officers and men and their families.

After luncheon the Royal Party toured displays of equipments and units on Alma Square. Displays were co-ordinated by Headquarters Combat Service Support Group (UK). The display commander was Colonel T.M Maccartney, who was supported by Major S J M Marriner, the Display Coordinator. The stands featured the Directorate of Clothing and Textiles, a 20 foot ISO container, Volvo with Trailer, Rail Transfer Equipment, Northern Ireland Explosive Ordnance Disposal, Base Stock,

ABOVE: Formation Parade in Dusseldorf (2 Group). BELOW: March past during the Cyprus Formation Parade. Commander British Forces Cyprus takes the salute.

Mobile Bath Unit, Field Laundry, Pioneer Labour Support Unit, Local Resources Section, Fork Lift Truck, Mini Mexeflote with simulated ammunition, Coles Crane with 20 foot ISO container, Simple Rail Transfer Equipment, Air Despatch Equipments, a Demountable Rack Off-loading Platform System, Bulk Fuel Installation and a Chemical Laboratory Assistant, a Pioneer Quick Reaction Force, Ammunition Preparation, Pioneer Decontamination Area, an Allied Command Europe Mobile Force (Land) Field Post Office, Fuel Tanker with Unit Bulk Refuelling Equipment, 5 Airborne Brigade Cameo, Commando Cameo, Immediate Replenishment Group, Transportable Stores Container and COFFER (Computerized Office for Field Force Enquiries and Records), and Field Catering.

Units represented in the displays were the Directorate of Land Service Ammunition, Directorate of Clothing & Textiles, Army School of Catering, Commando Logistic Regiment, 3 Close Support Regiment, 5 Airborne Brigade Logistic Battalion, 9 Supply Regiment, 17 Port & Maritime Regiment, 23 Pioneer Regiment, 27 Transport Regiment, 19 Tank Transporter Squadron, 25 Freight Distribution Squadron, 47 Air Despatch Squadron, 81 Postal & Courier Squadron, 518 Pioneer Squadron, 383 Commando Petroleum Troop (V), Mobile Field Laundry (V), the RLC Mobile Display Team, Vehicle Depôt Ludgershall, Regional Depôt Thatcham, Petroleum Centre Westmoors and the Army Fire Service.

A Tea Party was held in the Corporals' Mess at the end of the afternoon at which, once again, the Colonel-in-Chief met members of the Corps and their families. The afternoon ended with a visit to Regimental Headquarters, where the serving and retired officers were introduced and HRH met the Colonels Commandant. The finale of a long and outstandingly successful day was a Dinner Night held in the Headquarters Officers' Mess.

**Formation Parade**. The Princess Royal has asked me to write and thank you and the members of her Corps for a most enjoyable and interesting day on the occasion of the inauguration of The Royal Logistic Corps.

Her Royal Highness appreciates tremendously the amount of planning and hard work that is needed to produce such an excellent parade, as well as the displays, not to mention an interesting tour of the museum and the delicious meals. Her Royal Highness has asked that her warmest thanks and congratulations are passed on to everyone involved, in particular Colonel Lake, Lieutenant Colonel Taylorson, Major Ward and Sergeant Major Robinson. Her Royal Highness was delighted to have the opportunity of both meeting members of her Corps and learning a little of their roles that make up such a vital and important part of the British Army.

The Princess was very touched by the warm welcome that she received from everyone and as Colonel-in-Chief wishes me to pass on her very best wishes for the future to all ranks serving in her Corps.

*A letter from Lady in Waiting to the Director General.* *7 April 1993*

**The Royal Visit.** With a great deal of trepidation, I found myself leaving Cyprus for the slightly less sunny climes of Deepcut, to take post as Project Liaison Warrant Officer for the Royal Visit of HRH The Princess Royal for the Corps Formation Parade. One of the first shocks to my system was the amount of work involved – it was far from the 'cushy' number I had had described to me prior to taking post. What do I remember of the birth of The Royal Logistic Corps? Two words come to mind: photograph and itinerary.

Photograph: I had the dubious honour of appearing in the June 1993 *Corps Journal* carrying (or juggling) a pacestick, radio, mobile phone and a regimental umbrella. That particular piece of history is courtesy of Colonel Lake as he thought it amusing that I should be attempting to carry all the above whilst in the Her Royal Highness' party. He had previously expressed a wish to get a photograph for the *Journal*, which I quickly declined; however, he assured me that before

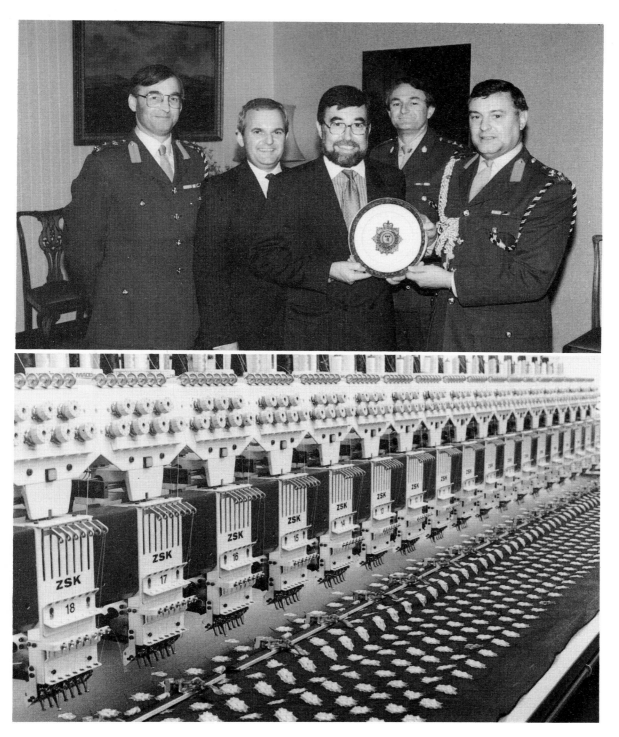

ABOVE: Presentation to the Corps by Royal Doulton, 1994. BELOW:
Corps cloth badges during the manufacturing process.

the day was out he would have his photo. Needless to say, it happened just as we were going into the Explosive Ordnance Disposal display and I was looking the other way. This accounts for my pose *au naturel*.

Itinerary: part of the dictionary definition is *'route; record of travel; guidebook'*. What it does not say is that it demands a painstaking time appreciating, coordinating and orchestrating almost every minute of a visit. This is magnified for a Royal Visit. If you have never done an itinerary for a Royal Visit before, a word of advice ... don't! I still have a copy, all fifty-two pages of it.

For me the Formation Day was one of the only times I got to sit in a grade one staff car and have people wave at me, or more precisely the Royal Party, was able to refuse a General entry to a stand (General Wilsey) and to meet many different people far senior and junior to me. So what did I get from the visits?

*Experience:* a one off appointment never to be repeated. *Fame:* everyone is famous for five minutes – I think I had mine during the visit, but was too busy to notice. *Friendship:* I have never met such a hardworking purposeful team in my career, each and every one of them 'deserves a medal. *Achievement:* on a job well done. *Relief:* that the visit was over. *Sadness:* at saying farewell to a cohesive and effective team. No words I have could thank them for their time, effort and dedication, much of it into the wee small hours!
*Warrant Officer One (Regimental Sergeant Major) M D Robinson, 9 Supply Regiment.*

**Formation and Medal Parade, Split; 4 April 1994.** The fateful day had eventually arrived, the moment every true blue Royal Army Ordnance Corps officer and soldier had dreaded: the end of the Corps. My last moments in the Royal Army Ordnance Corps and the first in The Royal Logistic Corps were spent in Shed 5 at Split Port, standing to attention waiting for the presentation of my United Nations medal. It actually crossed my mind as to why we were parading in this icebox of a storage shed, instead of in the nice

warm Adriatic sunshine not more than five feet away.

Once the parade finished we duly handed back our medals. It appeared that there were not enough to go around: The Royal Logistic Corps' first real logistic problem.

The enormity of what had taken place that April only really struck home on return to Germany. The Royal Logistic Corps was everywhere and this struck me most when I saw the Corps stable belt in every camp I went to.
*Captain P W Edwards, 93 Petroleum Squadron.*

**An Early Dawn and a Late Parade.** In Cyprus the formation of The Royal Logistic Corps was foreshadowed a year early when it was decided to act upon the recommendations of the Logistic Support Review report and re-organise the logistic support given to British Forces Cyprus.

The Cyprus Logistic Unit was formed in April 1992 with its Headquarters at RAF Akrotiri. It consisted of Royal Engineers (23 Postal & Courier Squadron), Royal Corps of Transport (Transport and Movement Squadron), Royal Army Ordnance Corps (Supply Company and Ration Company) and Army Catering Corps (Central Catering). The Royal Air Force were incorporated with their Supply Squadron. The Royal Pioneer Corps were not included as they had a Defence Pioneer Platoon under command of 9 Signal Regiment.

5 April 1993 dawned early for the Commanding Officer Cyprus Logistic Unit, Lieutenant Colonel Charlie White, as he moved across the command by helicopter to present the new cap badges. In the afternoon, in the eastern Sovereign Base Area, a beach barbeque was held for all Royal Logistic Corps soldiers and their families.

For the Cyprus Logistic Unit the actual formation parade did not take place until 8 April 1993 as the new Commander British Forces, Major General A. G. H. Harley CB OBE, did not arrive on the island until 7 April. It was unfortunate that the day itself was wet and windy. The General's car did not appear

ABOVE: The Forming Corps Associations march past on the first Corps Sunday, 1993. LEFT: Lieutenant Colonel M E Wilcox buries a time capsule (16 Regiment); RIGHT: Officers of The Royal Logistic Corps at the Staff College on Formation Day 5 April 1993.

at the front of the parade as expected but arrived at the rear of the spectators and he had to pick his way through the crowd to the rostrum. He inspected the parade and presented five soldiers, representing the Forming Corps, with their cap badges. During the General's speech the Royal Air Force decided to land a Tristar on the adjacent runway so we shall never know exactly what his words of wisdom were.
*Cyprus Logistic Unit.*

**The Bank of China Building Saw it All.** In keeping with the rest of the Corps, 29 Transport Squadron marked the birth of The Royal Logistic Corps with a formation parade; however most similarities ended there and it is our claim to have been involved in one of the most unusual formation parades in the Corps.

Our first claim to fame is that the Hong Kong parade did not in fact occur on 'the day' at all. This was because the Corps Formation Day coincided in Hong Kong with a public holiday held in celebration of the Chinese Ching Ming Festival. As the majority of our manpower are Chinese soldiers from the Hong Kong Military Service Corps, most were already engaged on 5 April paying homage to their ancestors, tending the graves and cleaning the bones of their deceased relatives, as opposed to the rest of the Corps, who were engaged in bidding farewell to their predecessors. As a result the formation of the Corps in Hong Kong did not occur until 8 April.

Another difference, and surely a 'first' for any formation parade, was the presence on parade of the 29 Squadron Lion Dance Display Team, who provided a Lion Dance display to bring good luck to all participants and to the new Corps. The first duty of the reviewing officer, Commander British Forces, Major General J P Foley CB OBE MC, was to dot the eye of the lion, metaphorically to bring it and the new Corps to life.
*29 Transport Squadron, Hong Kong Logistic Support Regiment.*

**In Step With the New Corps.** I always considered myself to be a natural leader and I have always believed in leading from the front. Unfortunately for me, my feet have never agreed with this philosophy and have throughout my career continually let me down. The formation of The Royal Logistic Corps was one such occasion and it is true to say that I entered the new Corps completely out of step.

As part of 21 Regiment my squadron (on roulement) and I were duly called to take our place on The Royal Logistic Corps formation parade at Lisburn.

On the big day, the weather was kind to us and everything was ready. The order came to 'march on the officers' and I was off to take my position in front of my squadron. All was well so far: Brigadier Bob Bullock, the inspecting officer, presented new Corps cap badges to a selected number of soldiers and we were then ready for the big finish, the march off. The band of 152 (Ulster) Ambulance Regiment (V) struck up and I stepped off, confident that my first steps in the new Corps would be ones I would remember for a long time.

My feet as usual had other ideas and by the time we were approached the saluting dais my Sergeant Major had had enough. In a quiet voice just audible to me and most of the squadron Warrant Officer Two Brodie whispered, 'Well done, sir, you are the only one in step in the whole squadron'. With such loyalty how could The Royal Logistic Corps fail to go forward in perfect step in the future?
*Major M J Varley, 16 Tank Transporter Squadron.*

**The Journal.** Thank you for forwarding me a copy of the first issue of The Royal Logistic Corps *Journal*.

On behalf of my old Corps (328 years) and elderly magazine (we celebrated our centenary last year) may I wish you youngsters the best for the future, and extend you an invitation to visit us if you are ever in this area.

ABOVE: Signing the Letters Patent recording the link between the Corps and the Worshipful Company of Gold and Silver Wyre Drawers. Major General D L Burden CBE, Major General C E G Carrington CB CBE and Mr Roy Rutter, Master of the Worshipful Company of Gold and Silver Wyre Drawers. BELOW: St Barbara's Church, Deepcut.

I have added you to our mailing list so you should continue to receive *The Globe & Laurel* every two months. I hope you will enjoy reading it.

PS. I was delighted to see that you have chosen a Regimental March written by an ex-Royal Marine (and a bass player to boot).

*A letter to the Editor from the Editor*
*The Journal of The Royal Marines.* April 1993

Thank you for the first commemorative *Journal* of The Royal Logistic Corps and change of location information, which has been noted. The *Journal* was excellent in all respects.

May we take this opportunity to wish you every success with your publication in the future and not forgetting the inevitable sadness that will exist for many in losing their old cap badges. We hope the settling in period will be quick and effective.

Many congratulations from us all at *The Craftsman.*

*A letter from the Editor of The Craftsman.*
April 1993

**Blowing a Gale in Plymouth.** On the parade square at Seaton Barracks was a desperate place to be on 5 April 1993. Situated atop Crownhill, overlooking the City of Plymouth, the square is at the best of times a windswept place. This day was certainly no exception.

The regiment was stood at ease facing the dais. Once the non-RLC officers fell in and the Commanding Officer arrived, the regiment was brought to attention. Every man stood erect and still but with a noticeable lean to the left as the near gale force winds whistled constantly from left to right across the square.

Words were spoken by the Commanding Officer followed by a blessing from the unit Padre for the new Corps flag. It was then the turn of the senior Royal Logistic Corps officer present to speak, Colonel R E Ratazzi, Deputy Chief of Staff HQ Commando Forces Royal Marines. He took the dais and spoke

eloquently about the meaning of this important occasion to us as members of the new Corps. He spoke of the big reorganisation within the regiment. The rest of the speech was a somewhat blurred affair as by now it was raining heavily. The rows of Royal Logistic Corps ranks were still leaning to attention, individuals soaked to the skin on one side, the other side of them in bone dry Service Dress, such was the ferocity of the rain. On completion of his speech Colonel Ratazzi shook each man by the hand and presented him with a blue cloth cap badge, the only piece of Royal Logistic Corps uniform then available.

*Lieutenant A Madison, The Petroleum Centre.*

**'My Kingdom for a Motto.** (*Tutene! Atque cuius exercitus: Anon*) Corps mottoes rarely emulate the spirit of the body they represent. Given the options *'Nil sine labore'* (Nothing without Work), *'Sua tela tonanti'* (To the Warrior his Arms), *'Labor omnia vincit'* (Work 'Triumphs over Everything) or *'Ubique'* (Everywhere), 'We Sustain' is a relatively unprepossessing motto. Considering that 'to sustain' is 'to hold up, support, bear weight of, keep from falling or giving way, undergo or suffer', the uninitiated may be forgiven for thinking that The Royal Logistic Corps was a bunch of philanthropic strongmen. A liberated choice would have been *'Haud fiet, et clavi fixum est'* (Nothing doing, and that's final).

*Captain A F Peake, The Petroleum Centre.*

***Ubique*, but mostly at Mill Hill.** As Sappers, the Postal and Courier Services, have always valued their motto with pride. When The Royal Logistic Corps loomed 'everywhere' was beginning to look a bit like 'all over the place' ... some even muttered 'a bit of a bloody mess!'

How do you tell a soldier that he is no longer going to be a Sapper, even though Sappers were to continue in the Army? Not easy, especially with cries like 'Once a Sapper

ABOVE: The Colonel-in-Chief and senior officers at the Bicentenary Dinner in Deepcut, 2 November 1994. BELOW: Corps Dinner Night on 27 January 1994, with HRH The Duke of Gloucester present.

always a Sapper' being repeated by the die-hards. The officers were not a problem ... they were getting a grant of a tenner to buy a new mess kit.

The problem was solved with ruthless enthusiasm by Our Member of the Famous Five. Every single reference to the Royal Engineers was removed from Mill Hill in our equivalent of a Night of the Long Knives. Regimental history in the form of plaques, signs and mementoes all mysteriously disappeared in the two weeks leading up to the Big Day ... it was as if we had never previously belonged ... but were about to be welcomed with open arms into the Really Large Chest of a very caring foster mother. Parties and parades of celebration, not commiseration, were planned at all levels involving all staff, from the cleaners to the Chief Executive.

One has to say it worked ... the Really Large Chest has a warm feel to it. We wear our multi-coloured stable belts with pride, albeit under the jersey – for now at least. The memorabilia of our fond links with Sappers have returned and are proudly displayed and *Ubique,* ... well that is all but forgotten. *We Sustain* is fine and our own special logo, affectionately known as 'Birds and Bars', is just perfect. For the historical record the logo illustrates our aim to be 'Swift and Secure'.
*Postal & Courier Depot, Mill Hill.*

**United We Stand.** Contrary to military doctrine (most unusual for HQ BAOR), we had divided our forces in order to conquer the local units in the Rheindahlen area. Small but powerful detachments were sent into the field with instructions not to return until their mission was accomplished. The rest of us waited anxiously back at Rheindahlen, awaiting confirmation of their success, which was to be the signal for the opening of the champagne, for toasts, and breakfasting late into the morning.

Eventually the signal was given as our commanders returned: Commander Army Catering Services had captured the Junior Ranks' Mess, and in doing so converted (rebadged) five soldiers to The Royal Logistic Corps; likewise, Commander Postal & Courier Services emerged triumphant from the Sergeants' Mess. Commander Logistic Support (Brigadier Derek Williams), Commander Supply (Brigadier David Harris) and the other Branch Colonels had been present at both, and they all returned in good heart to B Officers' Mess, where the officers and their guests, including General Sir Charles Guthrie KCB LVO OBE (Commander-in-Chief BAOR), Major General P J Sheppard OBE (Chief of Staff BAOR) and Air Chief Marshall Sir Andrew Wilson KCB AFC RAF (Commander-in-Chief Royal Air Force) (Germany), had assembled. The regimental breakfast was more akin to a wedding breakfast, with toasts, speeches and messages of goodwill from afar.

Seriously, of course, the formation of the new Corps was very much a wedding, with the new partners giving much to the new family, and at the same time having to learn to live with new relatives. The impressions of all of us present in HQ BAOR at the time are that the detailed preparations leading up to the formation of the new Corps gave us all a firm base from which to step off. Much credit for this must go to Colonel Paddy Henderson and his 'Mr Fixit', Captain Frank Wenlock, and Lieutenant Colonel (Retired) Alan Knipe and his staff in the Secretariat. For most the first few days of the new Corps were 'business as usual', which, though unexciting to report, is exactly the effect that the Headquarters would have wished for. Two years on, we can say that this process has been a success; we now speak the same language, understand each other's problems and stand united.
*Logistic Support Branch, Headquarters United Kingdom Support Command (Germany).*

**The Bicester Perspective.** After the anxious parents had safely delivered the latest addition to the world there was a feeling of

ABOVE: Mounting Guard at Buckingham Palace in 1994 (10 Transport Regiment). BELOW: The Freedom of the Borough of Surrey Heath. Lieutenant Colonel N B Josling leads the March Past, with the salute taken by the Mayor of Surrey Heath (RLC Training Centre).

anti-climax. The worries and doubts which had existed and the complications of a different gestation period gave way to a natural and trouble-free birth. The specialist reported the safe delivery of a perfect new arrival, noting that the infant was larger than had been anticipated. The arrival of The Royal Logistic Corps had all the attractions of a splendid pedigree and already bore the hallmarks of a certain winner. At Bicester The Royal Logistic Corps had already existed in all but name. Elements of all the Forming Corps had worked together since the depôt's formation fifty years ago.

On Formation Day, 5 April 1993, the weather was not kind. A damp and overcast dawn saw the officers and senior ranks of 16 Battalion Royal Army Ordnance Corps gather at the guardroom of St George's Barracks to witness the raising of the Royal Logistic Corps flag. This was followed by a tour of the barracks to serve 'gun fire' to the rather sleepy soldiers, who proved somewhat reluctant recipients. After a regimental breakfast everybody was looking forward to the formation parade but the unpredictable British weather did not abate and a shortened parade had to be held in the garrison theatre.

The depot had been very much involved with the creation of The Royal Logistic Corps weeks in advance. The receipt into depôt stock of the new badges, buttons and embellishments and the eventual issue of these items worldwide had created additional work. The depot workshop had performed excellent service in the preparation and erection of the new depot signs and it is only at a time like this that one becomes fully aware of the myriad variety of signs in an area the size of Bicester Garrison. For the civilian staff of the depot this was perhaps the only physical sign that anything had changed, otherwise it was 'business as usual'.

For future generations a time capsule may be the only clue as to what happened at Bicester. This was buried by the Commanding Officer 16 Regiment, Lieutenant Colonel M E Wilcox, outside the regimental headquarters.

On 26 May 1993, to mark the formation of Royal Logistic Corps Postal Services, a British Rail Class 47 Locomotive was named *Royal Logistic Corps Postal & Courier Services*. The ceremony, which took place in Building D8 of 2 Sub Depot and was attended by many guests, was performed by Director General Logistic Support (Army), Major General D L Burden CBE. Sporting its new plates the locomotive then hauled an eleven coach passenger train with the guests on board to London Euston.And now, as we are at the second anniversary of our Corps, original individual misgivings are fading into distant memory and The Royal Logistic Corps at Bicester look forward to a future full of promise.
*Headquarters Bicester Garrison and Base Ordnance Depot.*

**The Military Secretary's Department.** With the formation of The Royal Logistic Corps, a new Personnel Branch, PB10, was formed at Stanmore, from the amalgamation of the staffs from PB8 (Royal Corps of Transport), PB9 (Royal Army Ordnance Corps), and that element of PB17 which looked after the Army Catering Corps, Royal Pioneer Corps and Royal Engineers (Postal & Courier Service) officers.

As at 5 April 1993, some twenty-two staff, fourteen military and eight civilians, were responsible for the career management and administration of 2203 officers. This sizeable organisation quickly felt the implementation of the decisions made in Options for Change and, two years on, the PB10 strength reduced to twelve staff, eight military and four civilians managing approximately 1800 officers. This reduction in officer strength was primarily as a result of a phased redundancy programme: sixty-six officers in 1993-94 and 221 officers in 1994-95. Particularly hard hit were those officers who held a Late Entry Commission. At the end of the redundancy programme The Royal Logistic Corps officer strength was some thirteen per cent of the Army's officers.

ABOVE: Painting of 18 Transport Squadron Royal New Zealand Corps of Transport in a rubber plantation in Malaysia, presented in recognition of their close affiliation with the Royal Corps of Transport. BELOW: RHQ The RLC and Forming Corps group at Arromanches plaque dedication, June 1994.

Apart from its sheer size, the complexities of the functions of a multi-disciplined Corps, where specialist and generalist appointments are intertwined, proved a major challenge. There were quite naturally worries about the ability of PB10 to ensure fair play and equity during the early years, particularly for Group B officers. Those fears were well acknowledged and transitional arrangements were implemented.

Having managed the significant changes involved with the formation of the Corps, the next major hurdle will be the formation of the Army Personnel Centre in Glasgow in 1996, when officer and soldier manning will come together in a new structure. An era will have come to an end, and Stanmore, which has looked after officers' careers since 1949, will pass into history. *PB10.*

**Manning the Changes.** The principal events which affected Royal Logistic Corps Manning & Record Office (North), the former Royal Corps of Transport Manning Record Office, on 5 April 1993 were the loss of the clerical trade and the Staff Band to the Adjutant General's Corps and Royal Logistic Corps Manning & Record Office (South) respectively, and the gain of the Postal & Courier operators from the Royal Engineers. To compensate for the remoteness of Glasgow from the main centre of the Corps' formation activities in the south of England, military officers in Glasgow marked the day with a noisy supper party at the OIC's house.

The transformation was not entirely uneventful. The computer was tasked overnight to change all Royal Corps of Transport soldiers to Royal Logistic Corps, but in the process all the Air Despatch trade disappeared from screen, thus 120 soldiers were electronically lost for three to four weeks. Fortunately no-one told them of this sad development.

One thing that does not change, however, is the soldier whose career we manage, nor the Army's sense of humour, both of which

are illustrated in the extract from a letter show below:

'Thank you for Reference B. I am concerned that you consider "a number of points raised in Reference A are self-inflicted". As we have no control over Servicemen prior to their posting to this unit, this can only refer to our having had four drivers in fourteen months. We believe the reasons, too, were not entirely of our making. The first couldn't navigate his way out of the camp. The second was excellent, top of his B1 course, but unfortunately his wife was somewhat overactive and it was fortunate that a fresh regiment was arms plotted to keep up with the demand. The third was posted here quickly because he was compromisingly caught with his friend's wife. The fourth has four Royal Military Police reports following him and a conduct sheet reminiscent of a fairground pugilist. I am not surprised Lance Corporal...... did not object to his report. If he had stayed any longer he would have served the rest of his time in jail. Whilst this is now all historical, your inference of "self-inflicted" appears a touch unkind.'
*The RLC Manning & Record Office (North).*

**One Day's Pay Scheme.** Thank you for your letter of 28 January 1994 concerning my contribution to the One Day's Pay Scheme. Please accept my apologies for not replying sooner, however as I am now in Croatia your letter has taken some time to find its way to me.

I have just been advised that I am to be made redundant under Phase Three, consequently my finances will no doubt be placed under some strain in the coming difficult months. I regret that I will not be able to contribute to the scheme during my last year of service.
*A Royal Logistic Corps Officer*     *March 1994*

**The Journal.** As an old soldier, who enlisted in the Royal Army Ordnance Corps in 1930, I would like to congratulate you on producing

ABOVE: The Colonel-in-Chief naming The Princess Royal Barracks, Gutersloh. BELOW: Laying up of Forming Corps flags in Dhekelia (Cyprus Logistic Unit).

65

such a first class Royal Logistic Corps *Journal*. You have certainly maintained the high standard which the old Royal Army Ordnance Corps *Gazette* set.

The coloured photographs of Her Royal Highness The Princess Royal as Colonel in Chief of The Royal Logistic Corps and the two Deputy Colonels in Chief are excellent and the historic formation in April 1993 of the new Royal Logistic Corps at Deepcut in the June issue of your *Journal* is extremely well covered. Well done.

May I wish you continued success in the future.

*Letter from a retired Association member*

*August 1993*

**What's in a Name?** In the days leading up to and immediately after the formation of The Royal Logistic Corps I was serving as the Admin Officer of Headquarters Squadron, Regimental Support Unit Bicester. Prior to 1993 the unit had been known as 16 Battalion RAOC, a title that went back to July 1942. You can imagine what the Commanding Officer, Lieutenant Colonel M. E. Wilcox, thought of the new unit title. Hardly the sort of name to inspire young soldiers to have pride in their unit.

Time was spent during 'prayers' discussing possible new titles for the unit. Representations were made to various agencies requesting support in the bid to rename the unit with a title soldiers would be able to identify with and be proud of. Alternative titles were put forward up the chain of command and reaction awaited.

In the meantime the Commanding Officer decided on a further measure to keep the title '16' alive. He tasked the PRI Officer (yours truly) with investigating the feasibility of purchasing, in quantity, a small embroidered badge. The badge was to be in Royal Logistic Corps blue with the number 16 embroidered in Roman numerals. To offset the cost the badge would be issued to soldiers and purchased by Senior NCOs and officers.

The Commanding Officer's efforts were eventually rewarded on 5 August 1993 with the unit being officially granted the title 16 Regiment Royal Logistic Corps and the badge is now proudly worn by all members of the unit.

*Captain C A Walker, 16 Regiment.*

**Life Goes On At the Top.** Base Ammunition Depot Kineton is situated in south Warwickshire between Banbury and Royal Leamington Spa. It has been a functioning ammunition depot since 8 October 1942, comprising two sub-depots, Edgehill and Marlborough. The depot covers approximately eleven square kilometres and has an inventory worth £850 million.

The manning is split between civilian and military personnel. Royal Logistic Corps units with the depot environment are: BAD Kineton, 92 (Ammunition) Squadron, 614 Troop and a 23 Pioneer Regiment detachment. The depot changed its title from Central Ammunition Depot to Base Ammunition Depot.

The unit has continued to send personnel to support operations in Northern Ireland, Bosnia and other overseas deployments. Sporting achievements since the formation of The Royal Logistic Corps have included Army Football Minor Unit Cup winners 1994, Army Minor Unit runners-up 1993, West Midlands Inter-Services Football League (WMISFL) Premier League winners 1993-94, WMISFL Cup winners 1993-94, Royal Logistic Corps Minor Units runners-up 1994, Wales & Western District Cup winners 1993-94, Army Team Marathon champions (Minor Units) 1994, finalists Army Athletic Championships 1994, Army Minor Unit Athletics champions 1993, Wales & Western District Minor Unit winners, London District Minor Unit winners, Royal Logistic Corps Minor Unit and Overall Champions. *Base Ammunition Depot Kineton.*

**Honorary Degrees in DIY.** Although 5 April 1993 was the official day that 3 CS Regiment was born and placed on the map, the process had started in earnest back in January 1993. By the end of February the

LEFT: Forming Corps flags laid up in Ambrosden Church (HQ Bicester Garrison and Base Ordnance Depot); RIGHT: Corporal Chow Kuen soars through the flames (29 Transport Squadron). BELOW: Mobility, Kathmandu style: Warrant Officer Two Tressler, Staff Sergeant M J C Heard, Major K N F McGowan, Major N F G Brehaut and Lieutenant Colonel P A C Gilham (Headquarters British Gurkhas Nepal).

67

regiment looked well set up. Of course the changes were far more extensive than the alteration of names. Whilst the Famous Five in Andover watched the dust of the amalgamation settle, life down in the weeds was more dynamic, and certainly frenetic.

On the formation of 32 Brigade Support Squadron there were but seven people in the station, comprising two Captains and five soldiers. Omitted from the special instructions paragraph of their posting orders was the requirement to be qualified to operate bolt croppers, hammers and screwdrivers and to have an irreducible sense of humour. For the first few months of the squadron's existence this small band of merry men built desks, painted walls, fixed roofs, laid carpets, chiselled off pigeon droppings and generally made the area look presentable, even if it remained only partially habitable. By Formation Day, with the squadron strength exceeding one hundred, the proud original 'magnificent seven' were presented with their honorary degrees in DIY as the assembled masses viewed the gleaming, smart new squadron working accommodation.
*3 Close Support Regiment.*

**Did the Workshop Notice?** The Logistic Support Battalion AMF(L) was largely unaffected by the furore leading up to the formation of the new Corps. This was not a result of apathy or indifference across the ranks, but simply a recognition that little would change for us. For the best part of two decades the battalion had been multi-functional in logistic terms, comprising transport, supply and equipment support sub-units, all with clearly defined and integrated roles in support of the ACE Mobile Force (Land).

Allegiance to the parent Corps, quite evident during competitions within the battalion for sporting and military skills trophies, was always subordinate to battalion loyalty. The battalion had its own black stable belt (black being the standard NATO colour for logistics) and unique insignia. It was always judged as a single entity on Force exercises, where the different cap badges had little significance for our NATO colleagues – we were all simply 'logisticians'.

Nonetheless, on 5 April 1993, it was an interesting experience to be wearing the same cap badge as our colleagues from other Corps but, in the true spirit of the battalion, we were not sure that the AMF(L) Workshop even noticed.
*The Logistic Support Battalion Allied Command Europe Mobile Force (Land).*

**A Dream Fulfilled. A Thousand Miles Away. Thoughts on Formation Day.** The first day in April. All over the world soldiers were busy preparing for the formation of a new corps, for on the fifth day in April The Royal Logistic Corps would come into existence. I, however, was a thousand miles away from this frenzied activity, both physically as well as metaphorically. Rather than prepare for the formation, I spent the months prior to April preparing to climb a mountain in Alaska. Eight men, from a variety of Corps and regiments, had departed that morning, heading for Anchorage, Alaska, and then on to the Danelaw National Park.

On Formation Day itself I was leading our eight man team on a one hundred mile ski approach to our objective, Mount Forager. The thought of the thousands of boots crunching across parade grounds all over Great Britain and Germany could not have been further from my mind. The towering massif of Mount Forager loomed menacingly in front of us, demanding our complete attention.

I stood on top of 'my' mountain on the 26 April. The pleasure was fleeting, however, as wind chill temperatures of almost minus one hundred degrees centigrade drove us from the summit. The descent was long and traumatic, with bad weather, avalanches and frost bite chasing us down the mountain. There were no feelings of conquest. It was very much as if the mountain had allowed us to tread on its summit and was now reminding us how frail we really were. We

ABOVE: 66 Squadron farewell parade in Tidworth (10 Regiment).
BELOW: Supacats at work on Exercise Gryphon's Flight 1993 (15 Logistic
Support Squadron).

had climbed the Archangel Ridge, only the second expedition ever to climb Mount Forager via that route.

Arriving back in the United Kingdom at the end of May felt a little like Alice stepping through the looking glass. A great many changes had occurred and the fledgling Royal Logistic Corps was almost two months old. I still did not even possess a Corps badge, but I had fulfilled a dream.

*Lieutenant P J Edwards, The Petroleum Centre.*

**A Growing Tribute.** Days before the formation of The Royal Logistic Corps, in the depths of the Lincolnshire countryside, at the top of a cold and windy hill in Prince William of Gloucester Barracks, Grantham (PWOG for short but not yet an approved abbreviation in Joint Services Pamphlet 101) yours truly was called before the Adjutant. These were difficult times for us all. The Adjutant for the last few months had been one Captain Simon Bennett, a capable likeable and thrusting kind of chap, with years of service, shortly to be replaced by Captain Alex St Matthew-Daniel, the sort who requires no public address system for parades, is fresh from the Junior Command & Staff Course and runs a particularly rapid battle fitness test. Having briefly met Captain St Matthew-Daniel during a flying visit, Captain Bennett was sitting behind the desk, so one approached the office with caution and a large amount of flexibility.

'As you are acting parade Adjutant, old boy', (Simon was a smart lad, his service dress was in the tailor's shop still, so I was nominated; and he did not have an incontinent, halitosine dog either) 'the Commanding Officer has decided the regiment will commemorate the amalgamation with an enduring and lasting botanic tribute to the five Corps.' I quietly congratulated myself on the feat of lateral thinking which led my razor sharp brain to conclude that this would essentially consist of planting five trees on the lawn outside RHQ, one for each Forming Corps.

On the appointed day and at the appointed hour the Adjutant could be seen coaxing the chosen five trees into their holes prior to the parade and hoping that they would remain respectably vertical throughout the proceedings (a case of the Two Hat Syndrome popularised by Mayors and MPs now endorsed by the Treasury).

The criteria for selecting the species of trees to represent the individual Corps are either lost in the mists of time or Top Secret because one cannot persuade a soul to reveal why they were chosen.

*Captain J Paterson, Petroleum Centre.*

**The RLC Two Years On. How it Really Happened.** Sufficient time has probably now passed to make it safe to disclose the true facts surrounding the creation of The Royal Logistic Corps. For example, did you know that The Royal Logistic Corps originally comprised of four officers and one Senior NCO deployed without furniture in a conference room in Building 200 at the then Logistic Executive (Army) in Andover? Did you know that the Secretariat tasked to form The Royal Logistic Corps produced a subversive news sheet throughout the period of the new Corps formation? Or, that the whole process of forming up the Corps took eleven months? Read on ...

It is always important to start with a bit of history and it is a measure of the Corps' swift rise to maturity that the period of the Logistic Support Review through 1990-1991, rather like the Gulf War, really is now ancient history. In essence, the Logistic Support Review had reached a number of key conclusions by late 1991. These had been endorsed and Major General Carlier, Team Leader of the study, had produced follow-on papers to implement them. But it has to be said that the key findings were properly concerned with principle and needed some flesh on the bones before a new Corps, formed from five existing Corps, could be organised in the sort of detail that would ensure that its new members would have

ABOVE: Dodge EOD vehicle after being attacked with a Mk 16 Provisional Irish Republican Army improvised mortar (321 EOD Squadron). BELOW: 321 EOD Squadron in Northern Ireland, 1994.

such vital matters as a trade structure, organised units and equipment to go to when it formed.

For a while, the problem of translating principle into detail seemed insurmountable, until the Directors General and Directors of the existing Corps suggested to the Quartermaster General that the answer might be a Secretariat staffed by members of the existing Corps but working to the Quartermaster General to carry out the staff work needed to form the new Corps. This proposal coincided with the arrival of General Sir John Learmont as Quartermaster General and he determined to have one staff officer on his staff to implement the Logistic Support Review, Brigadier Chris Burson, late Royal Artillery, who became Director of the Logistic Support Review Implementation Team, with under him two key staff organisations: a Secretariat to deal with the reorganisation of the Quartermaster General's own staff and the Andover estate, and another, the Logistic Support Policy Secretariat, under the command of a Colonel to deal with the implementation of the Logistic Support Review insofar as it affected The Royal Logistic Corps. This Secretariat's task was to deal with all aspects of forming the new Corps, less those involving regimental matters – dress, custom, regimental funds and the like, which would be taken on by the early appointment of a Regimental Colonel, Colonel Mike Lake. Even excluding these matters, the Secretariat's remit was a wide one and ran through organisation, operational planning, establishment work and training issues. ('You name it, we will have to do it,' said the first luckless SO3.)

The Secretariat formed in double quick time at Andover on 5 January 1992. Colonel Graham Ewer had returned from HQ 1 (UK) Armoured Division in June 1991 at the end of the Gulf War to take over the School of Transportation in Aldershot and he was selected to lead the Secretariat. This team comprised Lieutenants Colonels drawn from each of the cap badges coming together into the new Corps who brought to it their particular expertise and experience. Lieutenant Colonel Alan Taylor, who had served with Colonel Ewer during the Gulf War, brought to it expertise in Royal Army Ordnance Corps matters. Lieutenant Colonel Paul Morris came from Postal & Courier, Lieutenant Colonel Duncan Robertson covered Catering, and Lieutenant Colonel John Allen, who joined slightly later, represented the Royal Pioneer Corps. Lieutenant Colonel Paul Fraser joined to cover Management Strategy and Lieutenant Colonel Jerry Lewis US Army covered doctrine, and kept order. Major Jeff Little was extracted from a posting to the School of Transportation and joined as the lead policy SO2 with first Captain Bruce Hosking, and then later Captain Nick Pratchek, as his Staff Officers Grade 3 and Staff Sergeant Browell as the sole military clerk.

In the first instance, the Secretariat formative process might have seemed to lack that certain sense of history and style which its members might have been led to expect. Our first accommodation, the then Ord 5 conference room in a corridor with REME in Building 200, proved amusing. It was big enough for all of us if it had no furniture, but the acquisition of furnishings produced the opposite effect and an immediate overflow problem. We were forced to leave some individuals in place if they already had an office in Andover, whilst the new boys who had no office in Andover made do with what we had.

From small beginnings, much bigger things came. We embarked swiftly on a war of manoeuvre around Building 200 in Andover, eventually seizing a piece of defensible territory in what had been Transport 2. In practice those already in possession of ground proved charitable, which was helpful since we had a great deal to do in short order. In particular, there was no coherent implementation plan for the new Corps and key policy areas for resolution were not identified.

Life in January 1992 had a distinct challenge to it, at least for the Secretariat, but we quickly

LEFT: Dulmen Inter-Services Marathon winners 1993; RIGHT: B Nations Ski-bob World Champion Lance Corporal Michelle Turner (99 Postal & Courier Squadron) with Colonel D A Den-McKay OBE. BELOW: The team captain of Base Ammunition Depot Kineton's 1993 successful athletics team gets his due rewards.

found that we were in a privileged position. The Quartermaster General personally was absolutely committed to the rapid and effective implementation of the Logistic Support Review and set up a clear Logistic Support Review Steering Group structure, chaired by himself and bringing together the Directors General and Directors of the then existing Corps in a forum which could give us clear direction and decide what action was to be taken. Equally important, the staffs of the existing Corps were on side. And it has to be said that those involved in the marriage knew each other well – many officers and soldiers from all five Corps had been working together to common purpose during the Gulf War only some ten months previously.

All this helped considerably. The Implementation Plan was written as required and on time. The fact that it grew to ten linked landscape pages did not matter overmuch once we were clear on the key phases to be executed in the time available. The key phases quickly became second nature – the absence of two of the ten pages for five weeks during one iteration of the plan was completely overlooked for at least six weeks with no apparent loss of momentum.

Midnight oil was a popular commodity in the early days. The Quartermaster General directed that the Secretariat should produce a series of baseline papers to establish a position and a plan for action in specific areas; for example, he directed that a paper should be written on the trade structure for the new Corps and we proposed a pragmatic way ahead so that changes could be implemented. Like papers were written for such diverse subjects as unit establishments, how training might be conducted, and the structure of Headquarters. To use the trade paper as an example, our key recommendation was that it was too late to make sweeping changes before the Corps formed and that the fairest solution for all those embodied into the new Corps would be to do so in their existing trades, with transitional arrangements following formation. This was accepted by the Logistics Support Review Steering Group and the

Secretariat then went ahead with the Director of Manning and his Manning and Record Offices to produce a manning plan with the right procedures to embody soldiers into the new Corps and retitle their trades on its formation, maintaining pay and qualifications. Most of these papers were successful in one way or another but some enjoyed a turbulent passage. Few areas proved more difficult than training, since the formation of The Royal Logistic Corps coincided with the creation of the Inspector General of Doctrine and Training and swingeing financial reductions.

As the months passed the purpose of the Secretariat began to be realised in full. It was our plan that the Secretariat should grow into the Logistic Support Policy staff branch, subsuming the tasks undertaken by the existing Corps staff branches. We were fortunate to inherit the establishment plan to achieve this. The year was marked by first the co–location of 'RLC' key staff individuals with existing staff branches, and then the eventual transfer of responsibility, a process which accelerated considerably once Major General David Burden was in place as Director General Logistic Support in September 1992.

With the Secretariat's increasing maturity came increasing complexity to our lifestyle. Logistic Support Policy 1(A) became the authors of a scurrilous news sheet, emulating perhaps the style of Sustainer, giving the real low-down on what was happening in Andover. The 'Dear Mum' column was much sought after and gave an up to the minute report on Andover high life.

A full scale ladies' guest night was organised on 27 August 1992, with Major General and Mrs Burden as the principal guests. This undoubtedly taxed the Andover Officers' Mess, as it did the participants during supper, who found their conversation across a twenty foot square table was a noisy business, demanding on the throat. A lack of common regimental custom in detail also proved interesting: the loyal toast producing scuffling as in a sizing parade at Pirbright.

LEFT: Corporal Anderson issues quick battle orders on exercise in Cyprus (23 Pioneer Regiment); RIGHT: Officers Petroleum Course, School of Petroleum Westmoors, 1994. BELOW: 17 Port & Maritime Regiment parade for New Forest Affiliation Parade, 1993.

If midnight oil had been the hallmark of the early days of the Secretariat, the presenter's rostrum became the symbol of its latter days as we dealt with the twin requirement to brief all those coming into the new Corps and to explain to the wider Army what the new Corps would look like and what it would do for them. Our plan was to conduct suitable presentations in tandem: the explanation of service to the wider Army preceding a more regimentally orientated presentation for those joining The Royal Logistic Corps. It has to be admitted that on some occasions the audience attended in reverse order, and one major headquarters overlooked entirely the need to invite those joining the Corps; however, the keen band of would-be volunteers from cap badges not joining The Royal Logistic Corps gave the forgotten few a good briefing afterwards. The team travelled extensively during the latter part of 1992, assisting with local plans for the introduction of the logistic support staff at every level.

The speed of all this development was striking. The team was small and very busy as a result but its small size increased performance since communication within the Secretariat was swift. Our close relations with the Forming Corps were invaluable, injecting much wisdom to solutions reached at every level. Acceptance of change was striking also. The process was gradual and some individuals were less happy with change than others. Speed towards the new Corps undoubtedly accelerated as time went by and as familiarity with new concepts increased. By December 1992 the Secretariat was effectively redundant. The new logistic support policy staff were in being and were shortly to take charge of affairs with the formation of The Royal Logistic Corps in April 1993. The Secretariat's tasks and staff were either moved elsewhere or subsumed in existing organisation. Some of those posted were sent away to implement the ideas they had spawned ... but that is another story.
*Improviser.*

## Time will Tell

The RLC is on its way
Design a cap badge by close of play
A bit too truckie it appears
To compound the other four's worse fears.

So off we go, cap badge and all
The RLC will have a ball
A huge new Corps has now begun
To challenge all and everyone

Truckie, Ordnance, Postie and Chefs
The Chunkies will make up the rest
The sporting scene must now beware
The RLC are everywhere

A hundred trades together all in one big
    group
A chef delivers letters, A Chunk will make the
    soup
A Truckie bomb disposal expert on the streets
    at last
A Pet Op Port and Maritime: now 'aint that
    just a blast?

What cap badge were you then before you
    had the chop?
What do you mean? The best of course, before
    the standards dropped
We'll put up with the others until they know
    the score
It might not be so bad, though, this Royal
    Logistic Corps

And have they got the balance right, those
    MOD type blokes?
Or is the Corps just too darn big, too chunkie
    you might say?
Time will tell. We'll all find out another future
    day!

*Headquarters Belize Logistic Battalion*

ABOVE: Chef: 'This meat tastes like old boots'. 'Yes, Sir, it is'. (8 Artillery
Support Regiment). BELOW: Catering Troop, Queen's Royal Hussars.

# REGIMENTAL AFFAIRS

In late 1991 the Quartermaster General endorsed the appointment of a Regimental Colonel to take post in March 1992. The task was to supersede earlier committees working on the myriad of issues collectively known as regimental affairs and to establish policy and the means for practical application in time for the formation in April 1993. A key aspect of this work would be to establish and form a Regimental Headquarters (RHQ).

The selected officer, Colonel Mike Lake, duly arrived on posting from Germany and made the early decision to locate the RHQ at Deepcut. In reality this meant finding an office, telephone and desk within the territory of the RAOC Training Centre and specifically within the building occupied by HQ RAOC(TA). From this initial base he undertook a subtle exercise in expansion and acquisition to create the offices and staff that now, two years on, constitute a most impressive and capable RHQ that befits a Corps as large, complex and ubiquitous as The Royal Logistic Corps

From the somewhat simplistic and vague task statement the real breadth of the problem emerged – it was like watching an iceberg turn downside up. As in most things the real grind was in the detail and practicality and much that had been previously signed and sealed proved more complicated in the delivery stage.

An early priority was to find helping hands. In its future moments of reflection the Corps should be grateful for the enthusiasm and loyalty to the new cause of Lieutenant Colonel Philip Taylorson (Corps Recruiting and Liaison Officer and SO1), Colonel (Retired) Mike Procter (Treasurer) and Lieutenant Colonel (Retired) John Hambleton (Secretary), all of whom continued to carry the burden of their existing jobs for some time while taking on the rapidly expanding business of the new Corps. The early team was strengthened subsequently by Lieutenant Colonel (Retired) Mike Young as Editor and Captain (Retired) Dick Mutch as Administrative Officer, WO1 K P Maloney as

Regimental Warrant Officer and many others in supporting roles.

There was much by way of sound example in regimental matters to draw on from the antecedents, or Forming Corps as they became known, and equally, unrivalled opportunity to develop fresh approaches. A fundamental decision, endorsed at an early stage by the Quartermaster General was the statement of ethos that from then on would govern the direction of development. In brief, this statement described The Royal Logistic Corps as based on a regimental structure with a predominantly field force nature. Another pivotal decision was that the Forming Corps would retain responsibility for their own Old Comrades and in the main, less a number of generous endowments to the new Corps, ownership of their property. This decision resulted in the broad organisation of the RHQ, with the inclusion of regimental offices for each of the Forming Corps to work in concert with the administration of The Royal Logistic Corps and in the style and content of trustee documents enabling the new Corps to hold property in trust.

The Corps inherited in trust an enviable collection representing the history of its antecedents in two main categories. The museum collections were combined in a rudimentary fashion in time for 5 April 1993, masterminded by the Curator, Lieutenant Colonel (Retired) Bill Masterson, and the Assistant Curator, Mr Frank O'Connell, with plans for relocation to a new build already in hand. This aspiration involved forceful and imaginative work on the part of the Regimental Headquarters staff and, as a result of the early retirement of the Curator, that of the Assistant Curator, and comes to fruition in June 1995 when the Colonel-in-Chief opens the museum in its new location.

It was immediately apparent that the key to the effective prosecution of regimental affairs would lie in the establishment of a strong and secure regimental fund and an uncluttered means of using those funds to the best effect. The new Corps, because of its size, had the

ABOVE: '. . . and then a little walk in the Dolomites'. 63 Airborne Close Support Squadron on Exercise Moulin Peak, 1993. BELOW: Support Battalion HQ ARRC on Exercise Handy Quadrant in Canada, 1993.

potential to generate and accumulate wealth quickly, but success would depend on the launch of a Day's Pay Scheme. The example of a notable amalgamation that had recently occurred was not encouraging and so this project was given special emphasis and effort, as it turned out, to significant effect. The committee structure to control regimental funds was devised so as to give majority influence to the serving Corps, while drawing benefit from the great experience available amongst the retired element of the Corps and its antecedents on functional committees.

The next stage was to plan for the effects of amalgamation on officers, soldiers and civilian employees. It was concluded that 'the means to inspire *esprit de corps* and regimental confidence would be vital to eventual success and this involved a breadth of work necessary to provide symbols and devices to demonstrate its identity and publications to communicate throughout its breadth and depth. The detail was frustrating, vexatious and often controversial, but the necessary goods were supplied to a surprisingly successful extent and in a timely and cohesive manner. A first Corps *Journal* was produced for Formation Day and the first issue proper was distributed soon after. The key ingredient, however, was to be the role and infectious enthusiasm of the Colonel-in-Chief, Her Royal Highness The Princess Royal, and of the Deputy Colonels-in-Chief, His Royal Highness The Duke of Gloucester GCVO and Her Royal Highness The Duchess of Kent GCVO. Their power to inspire unity was seminal and bringing this influence to bear in a practical way throughout the Corps as quickly as possible was a priority.

A further factor was the consideration that the future strength of the Corps would depend to an increasing extent on the recruitment of officers and soldiers and the work of the CRLO staff. It was necessary to devise a corporate image with the appropriate presentational material to enable them to attract recruits without a significant drop in quality or numbers. Furthermore, the message at all levels had to be the same and a new structure for liaison and coordination had to be created. This was all achieved without noticeable disruption and the Corps established itself quickly as a force in the recruiting market.

This summary is neither all-embracing nor does it begin to reflect the pace or magnitude of work involved as the Forming Corps quickly reached the point at which, immediately prior to the formation date, they had effectively handed the reins of leadership and management to the new administration. Some of the detail is best revealed in the individual and unit impressions that follow. These reflect the breadth of the task and the fact that the formation was effected without a noticeable break in support to the Army. Where letters have been used we have not published names but we thank all those who wrote to us on all subjects and from all countries.

Finally the process of change in a major corporation is complex, turbulent and potentially damaging to the goodwill and motivation of the employees. The amalgamation that resulted in the formation of The Royal Logistic Corps was unprecedented in the experience of a peacetime army and arguably the greatest undertaken by any single employer in the United Kingdom. The possibilities of only partially succeeding in the creation of a cohesive and efficient Corps abounded; nevertheless, the amalgamation has proved to be a resounding success because of the quality of our Servicemen and women and the emphasis given to winning their hearts and minds at an early stage.

*Factotum*

### First Meeting of the Colonels Commandant – 7 December 1992

A first meeting of the Colonels Commandant (Designate) was held at Deepcut on 7 December 1992 for the purpose of choosing a Corps Quick March. The following were present:

ABOVE: DROPS instruction for soldiers of 28 Squadron Queen's Own Gurkha Transport Regiment (10 Regiment). BELOW: Privates Vicky Gunner and Liz McGowan wobble their way across the drunken bridge (16 Regiment).

Colonel A F Barnett OBE
(Colonel Commandant Army Catering Corps)
Major General C B Berragan CB
Major General D F E Botting CB CBE
(Director General Ordnance Services)
Major General C E G Carrington CB CBE
(Colonel Commandant Royal Corps of Transport and Representative Colonel Commandant Designate)
Major General D B H Colley CB CBE
Major General G W Field CB OBE
Brigadier R J N Kelly CBE

The meeting was preceded by a musical presentation which included a number of compositions which were pre-selected for the occasion by the Regimental Colonel and the Directors of Music of the Royal Corps of Transport and the Royal Army Ordnance Corps Staff Bands. The selections included the quick marches of the Forming Corps; well-known marches not already ascribed to a particular corps or regiment and a compilation of Forming Corps marches scripted by Captain Stephen Smith. An opinion poll was recorded on conclusion of the presentation and the Colonels Commandant took note of these scores in their deliberations.

The Colonels Commandant met after the presentation and discussed each piece in turn and expressed their personal views. There was unanimous agreement that the marches of the Forming Corps should be discounted to avoid sensitivities but no clear concurrence emerged. The Colonels Commandant decided then to take supper with officers and take soundings. They reconvened after supper and reviewed their earlier discussions.

They reconsidered the earlier decision to exclude existing corps marches from their deliberations and decided by majority that it was appropriate to discard them. They took note of the opinion poll and of the views they had heard expressed by officers during the evening. They then voted as follows:

First    On Parade
Second  Something About a Soldier
Third    Blaze Away

Major General Burden, as future Director General, expressed his pleasure that a decision has been reached

*Extract from the minutes of the first meeting of the Colonels Commandant* *8 December 1992*

**Shop Items.** Further to our letter of the 10th instant we have pleasure to enclose herewith two sample headings in the Sports Colours crested ties design, one showing the shade of Gold 101 and one showing Yellow 59 for the motifs and stripes.

We would confirm that we have tried to match the gold shown on your striped ties as much as possible, however, should you require a darker shade please let us know and we will be happy to forward further samples for your approval.

You will see from the mounted sample headings that one shows the ties cut with a row of motifs at the bottom of the tie and the other with stripes only at the bottom. We wonder if you could please confirm which of these you require.

*The development of Corps ties with C H Munday Ltd* *December 1992*

## Dress – Specifications
The Royal Logistic Corps Badge
The colours to be used for the Corps badge are as follows:

*Crown*
Body and Framework – Gold
Pearl (Nine on each side arch and five on the front ar ch. Nine on the orb and one on each Maltese Cross) – White
Jewels – Red, White with five black tails
*Garter*
Strap – Blue
Edges of strap, tongue, buckle and lettering – Gold
*Axes*
Axe heads and shafts – Gold, lined black
Laurel wreath – Silver, lined black

ABOVE: Larger Corps — Larger Signs? (Theatre Drawdown Unit Germany). BELOW: Briefing for the drive to Denmark, 1994 (14 Transport Squadron).

*Shield*

    Cannon balls – Black

    The Chief (background to cannon balls) – Silver or White

    Cannons – Gold

    The Pale (background to cannons) Light Blue

*Scroll*

    Background – Gold

    Underside – Gold

    Lettering and border – Black

Colour specifications to be used in the reproduction of The Royal Logistic Corps badge using the lithographic printing process (paper, card) are taken from the Pantone Colour Scheme and are:

Red 185, Green 335, Light Blue 2985, Blue 280.

*Extract from the official specification for the Corps Badge*     *December 1992*

## Regimental Association Trustees

The following have agreed to become the first Trustees of the Regimental Association Trust Fund:

*Representative Colonel Commandant*
Major General C E G Carrington
*Director Logistic Support (Army)*
Major General D L Burden
*Director Logistic Support Policy*
Brigadier R M Bullock
*Commander Logistic Support United Kingdom Land Forces*
Brigadier P A Flanagan
*Commander Logistic Support Germany*
Brigadier G D Williams
*Commander Royal Logistic Corps Training Centre*
Brigadier P A D Evans
*Regimental Colonel*
Colonel C M Lake
*Colonel of Volunteers*
Colonel M Hughes
*Regimental Sergeant Major Training Regiment & Depot*
Warrant Officer One (Regimental Sergeant Major) M J Higham
*Regimental Warrant Officer*
Warrant Officer One K P Maloney

The Committee will be chaired by the Director General and the following members of the Secretariat are to be present:

    Regimental Secretary: Lt Col (Retd) J G Hambleton MBE

    Regimental Treasurer: Col (Retd) M Procter

*Extract from the appointment of the original Trustees*     *January 1993*

**Book of Remembrance**

In memory of those members
of
The Royal Logistic Corps
who died in Service with the Army
while serving on operational duty
worldwide
Their names are recorded in this
Book of Remembrance

*An extract of the front page of the Book of Remembrance*     *April 1993*

**Button Up.** I am a collector of British Army cap badges, collar badges, shoulder titles and buttons. Would it be possible to purchase a set of your new regiment's insignia, if not could I have a photocopy so that I may know what they look like? I enclose sae for your reply.

*A letter from the general public*     *April 1993*

**Officer Recruiting.** Why do you keep on writing to me. I have already told you I do not want to join your corpse I only want to fly.

*A letter from a high flier*     *May 1993*

**Plum & Apple.** I spoke with you recently on the telephone concerning jam. My particular interest is in the famous plum and apple jam of the First World War.

I would dearly love to have a copy, if one exists, of any Military specification. With a commodity such as jam the recipe is open to adulteration in both fruit and especially sugar content. This gives me hope that one exists. When we spoke you did not hold out much hope, that your archives contained such a

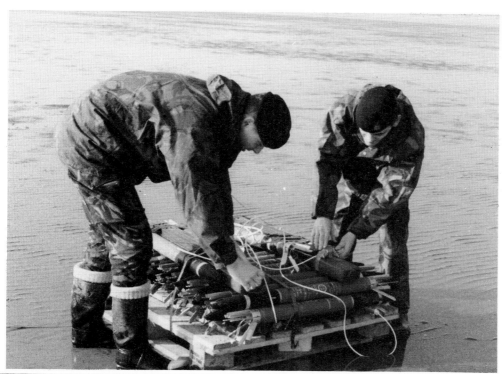

ABOVE: Laying demolition charges to destroy SNEB rockets (23 Pioneer Regiment). BELOW: Ramp powered lighter alongside in Belize — 'This is work, honestly!' (HQ Belize Logistic Battalion).

document. I would be extremely grateful if you would make what you consider a reasonable effort to trace anything on the subject.

Please place this letter at the bottom of your heap of inquiries. I won't hold my breath for the reply. Many thanks.

*A letter from a member of the public*

**Corps Dinner.** Forgive me for taking an age but the inertia of our holiday is still with me; the brain is not yet working nor is the pen, but any guilt on my part is partly assuaged that by now you will be in Cologne for the BMW Open! May I just thank you for inviting me on Thursday last – it was a smashing evening and great fun to be back among old chums, the only sadness on such occasions being there is never enough time to talk to all of them.

*A letter after the first Corps Dinner Night from the Commandant Surrey Army Cadet Force to the Regimental Colonel*     *June 1993*

**Royal Luncheons**. I am not quite sure of my status at the Commanding Officers Luncheon on 3 June 1993 (guest, paying or what?) but felt that I had to write to someone and express my delight at the manner in which the function was organised and the excellence of the luncheon itself.

Of course my great regret is that I have now had my one and only chance but the day is clearly something for others to look forward to. I would ask that you pass on my appreciation to those concerned.

*A letter from an officer after the first Commanding Officers lunch with the Colonel in Chief. June 1993*

**Church Kneelers.** Upon formation of The Royal Logistic Corps our Padre, Reverend E P Mosley Royal Army Chaplains Department, contacted Messrs Jacksons to procure a

Kneeler to supplement those already obtained for each of the Regiments/Corps/Arms who serve or have served on the Range. Jacksons respond that they have been unable to obtain coloured copies of The Royal Logistic Corps badge and background, which we presume to be blue.

We would be grateful if you could forward the necessary detail to:

Jacksons of Hebden Bridge
Croft Mill
Hebden Bridge
West Yorks
HX7 8AP

Alternatively there may be another manufacturer to whom you have already supplied this information, details of which you are in a position to provide.

*A letter to the RHQ from Senior Ammunition Technical Officer*
*Department, Isle of Benbecula*     *July 1993*

**Shop.** I would be very grateful if you could arrange to have six Royal Logistic Corps shields sent to me by return at the above address. Probably better to send two packets of three each in order to avoid problems with the diplomatic bag.

I note also that my Royal Logistic Corps Journal is not turning up. The only copy I have is that dated April 1993 – the inaugural issue. Of course it may be that we've gone `quarterly' and then I'll shut up!

Buenos Aires is a lovely city, full of parks and monuments testifying to its former glories. The people are friendly and, although I miss Deepcut terribly (cough!), I am enjoying flying the new Corps' flag here.

I do hope you don't think this a cheek but solving problems like this from here is not easy.

*A letter to the Regimental Secretary from a*
*Defence Attache in South America*     *July 1993*

LEFT: Corporal Gadsby (98 Postal & Courier Detachment) delivers mail to Vitez under Warrior escort. (Courtesy of *Soldier* Magazine) RIGHT: Bulk Fuel Installation Group One's guard commander, Bosnia (Britlogbat Op Grapple 4). BELOW: 94 Squadron arrives in Split, 1994 (9 Supply Regiment).

**Corps Club**. My day went off very well last Tuesday and I believe that you played no small part in its success. The Corps Silver on the table and the music played by the Corps pianist was indeed so unexpected and to say that I was flabbergasted would be to put it very mildly.

Thank you for the fine engraved plaque which I shall always treasure.

*A letter from a Club Secretary of one of the Forming Corps*           *July 1993*

**Dress Committee Minutes**
**Extract from Chairman's Briefing Notes**
**Item 4**
**Contentious Issues to be Resolved.** The attached list covers the dress matters that are particularly contentious and in need of resolution now. I suggest that you introduce the item by making a few points on ethos, Regimental pride and the importance of Corps identity to Officers and Other Ranks at more junior level.

I suggest you then take each item in turn. Stemming from discussion, there may be a need to add to interim arrangements.

**Stable Belt in Pullover Order.** There are mixed views on the wearing of stable belt in pullover order. Some clearly favour it being worn over the pullover to display the Corps Colour.

**Styles of Stable Belt.** There are at present two patterns of stable belt, a front buckle and a side strap. British Army of the Rhine has a policy whereby all ranks choosing to purchase a stable belt are to buy only the front buckle. This raises the question of return to England. Will individuals be allowed to continue wearing this pattern or be required to purchase the side strap variety?

**Officers' Lanyard**. Whilst reference is made to this item of dress in Item 6 it is worth mentioning. There are mixed views with regard to how it should be worn. When worn as for Dress Instruction it is bulky and spoils the cut of the Service Dress jacket.

Clarification on the wearing of female lanyard in Service Dress.

**Officers' Tie**. General comments are that it is bulky, difficult to tie neatly and loosens with wear. It costs between £19 and £22. Is it to be worn in No 13 Instructions?

**Mess Dress Trousers**. There have been many comments passed in regard to the new design Mess Dress. Most are complimentary when referring to the jacket and bib, however, the overalls/trousers have come under heavy fire. In particular the red stripes. Most unpopular across the Corps

**Korean Enquiry.** As the only surviving senior officer at the start of the British involvement on land in the Korean War in 1950, I have become involved in clearing our 27th Commonwealth Brigade Commanders home after the publication in USA in 1989 of *Disaster in Korea* by Lieutenant Colonel Roy Appleman. Major Alan Hunter – DAAQMG at Brigade HQ at that time – a Royal Army Service Corps officer – might be able to help me.

I would be grateful to be told whether he is still around and, if so, how I could get in touch, please. I will, of course, be happy to reimburse any expense incurred.

*A letter to the Regimental Secretary on historical matters*        *September 1993*

**Officer Recruiting.** Dear Lefthanded Colonel Taylorson, thank you for help in getting me a rail warrant to attend the Pre RCB in November I look forward to the course and meeting members of The Royal Logistic Corps.

*Letter received from a potential officer candidate*        *October 1993*

ABOVE: Charity Challenge team in action (9 Supply Regiment).
BELOW: Postal support for 5 Airborne Brigade, 1993 (29 Regiment).

**Officers' Club Tie**. Many thanks for the two Club ties which arrived this morning – they will certainly brighten up Ledbury and the surrounding area when I have occasion to dress up! I think they are smashing. (How about a bow tie – non-spinning?)

*A spontaneous tribute*       *October 1993.*

### Dress Regulations.

    Page A-1 – Suggest page should be J1-1
    Para 7 – Insert 'stockings' before tights.
    Para 8 – Delete in entirety
    – Insert 'The following may be worn:
    – Pearl stud earrings
    – Single or double short string pearl
      necklace
    – Watch
    – Wedding ring – if married
    – Engagement ring – if engaged
    – Eternity ring – if married'

*Draft Dress Regulation before the Dress Committee*     *October 1993*

### Dress for Royal Logistic Corps Officers and Soldiers.

The minutes of the last Royal Logistic Corps Dress Committee meeting issued on 15 October 1993, included a statement on the quality management/supply situation on various Royal Logistic Corps dress items. The impression given was that basically all is well. Unfortunately, I have to tell you that this is not so.

Leaving apart the WO1's No 1 Dress Hats, which you mention, we still have a problem in the British Army of the Rhine over the supply of a number of items such as small buttons, lanyards and collar dogs. We also have serious problems on the supply of mess kits and No 1 Dress hats for officers. The quality of many of the hats and some of the uniforms leaves much to be desired and in many cases the promised delivery dates are not being met.

*A letter from the British Army of the Rhine to the Regimental Colonel*     *November 1993*

### Association with the Worshipful Company of Gold and Silver Wyre Drawers.

I enclose a final draft for the Articles of Association which were cleared by the Gold and Silver Wyre Drawers Court on 4 October and have now been cleared by the Director General. I have added a paragraph which will allow the Master and General Burden to sign the document and to add a personal commitment to the Articles of Association.

I have had outline costings done and two documents, suitably prepared and encased within a sterling silver frame, will be about £1,400. I suggest we share the costs between us. Once you confirm that you are happy, I will go ahead with the arrangements.

Since drafting, we spoke today and I have now been in touch with Eric Pitchforth at the Tower of London, who has agreed to look at the calligraphic work involved and to be the focal point for the lunch. Once he has estimated the time scale he can work to, I will be in touch with some dates, but I think it is looking increasingly like January.

*An RHQ letter to the Company of Gold and Silver Wyre Drawers Liaison Officer*     *November 1993*

**Family Affair.** As part of my research into my personal family history, I am trying to locate a certain WO1 Tuddenham of the Army Service Corps who is known, via the Army Lists, to have served in WW1 in 1917. I have already tried to find him by way of the Medals Section of the PRO without success. They referred me to the Army Record Centre at Hayes in Middlesex and here, through the good offices of a friend living only 10 minutes away, I drew another blank. It appears that, with re-furbishment and an eye on security, that place is harder to get into than Fort Knox or HM Communications Centre, Cheltenham.

WO1 Tuddenham was, I strongly suspect, an uncle of mine but I know nothing of him other than that he carried some kind of silver

LEFT: Lance Corporal Kibble (left) Army and Inter-Services Triathlon Champion 1993, with Sergeant Dinwoodie who also represented Great Britain in the World Duathlon Championships in the USA (47 Air Despatch Squadron); RIGHT: Lieutenant Simon Hanford (27 Regiment), Winner of the Spirit of the Event Award at the Army Motor Cycling Championships, 1993. BELOW: The Silver Stars Parachute Team in competition over Netheravon, 1993.

topped swagger stick that he passed to my father. Any information you can give would be much appreciated. Failing this, can you recommend any further sources that might be useful. I enclose SAE for your response.

PS – From my own service record and knowledge of family traits, it just may be that the gentleman mentioned was not of unblemished reputation. Should you run across him for me, spare me nothing. It has always been a source of wonderment to me that some one of the name should achieve warrant rank.
*A letter from a correspondent in Nottingham*
*November 1993*

**Definition**. Since its inception, the British Army has operated a regimental system through which *esprit de corps* is encouraged. In the context of The Royal Logistic Corps the term regimental affairs is defined as `those matters which are controlled by the Corps itself, and the Trustees of Forming Corps Associations, subject to such regulations as the law imposes on trust and trust funds. They are distinct from manning and career management, or from those matters which are controlled by the Ministry of Defence as part of policies which are applicable to the whole Army, although such policies may impinge on the conduct of regimental affairs'.
*Extract from the Constitution of the Regimental Association. December 1993*

**Buttons and Badges.** Thank you for your letter of 10 December.

Our buttons were produced as a publicly funded item by the Directorate of Clothing and Textiles to a design agreed by the Famous Five. The contract was won in open competition between two firms, both major Ministry of Defence contractors.

I am sure that there is general dissatisfaction with the badges and buttons. A rather more up-market badge (and collar badge) is being looked at now and we may

see an improved appearance by 1995. We have yet to tackle the buttons but such is the pace of the process that I cannot imagine much happening before 1996.

Thank you for taking the trouble to write.
*A letter from the Regimental Colonel to a Commander Logistic Support of a District*
*December 1993*

**Journal Campaign**. I have just received the above and find it most interesting and informative, thank you and all the production staff.

Unfortunately, I have one complaint, on page 248 there is a picture of competitors in the British Army of the Rhine Athletic Championships. I am surprised that a Service Organisation does not know that there is a right and wrong way to display the National flag! It is upside down! The flagstaff end is on the right of the picture, therefore the broad white stripe is in the wrong place. It should be at the top. Flown this way is, as far as I am aware, a sign of distress! Are they in this situation?
*A letter to the Editor from a retired Association member.*
*December 1993*

**Mess Kit**. With reference to the above order for The Royal Logistic Corps Mess kit, please find enclosed a cheque for the full amount of £386.50. I received the kit this morning and am grateful for the speedy service. Many thanks!
*A satisfied customer*
*December 1993*

**Corps Dinner, Kensington Palace**. The Duke of Gloucester has asked me to thank you and everyone that was present at Dinner Night last Thursday for a most enjoyable and memorable evening.

His Royal Highness is particularly grateful to you and to General David for looking after him so well which all made such an enjoyable

LEFT: Private Ashton dipping the tanks (4 Squadron, 1 General Support Regiment); RIGHT: Warrant Officer One Tiffany and Lance Corporal Johnson at Vogelsang, 1993 (11 Support Squadron, 2 Close Support Regiment). BELOW: Corps members of HQ 1 (UK) Armoured Division, 1994.

and impressive evening and one which The Duke has said he will always remember.

His Royal Highness is also most grateful for the fine gold cufflinks which you so kindly presented at the dinner on behalf of The Royal Logistic Corps. This indeed was a lovely present and very unexpected and The Duke is delighted with them.

*A letter to the Representative Colonel Commandant from the Private Secretary to HRH The Duke of Gloucester*      *January 1994*

May I say what a great pleasure it was to enjoy such an excellent evening as your guest last night.

As I mentioned to you over Dinner, having witnessed the birth pangs of The Royal Logistic Corps, I think that the end result which is now up and running is something of which you can be justly proud. It would also be nice at this stage for some of your erstwhile detractors to see what a great success has already been achieved, which will clearly develop still further in the future.

Will you please also pass on my thanks to your colleagues for their very generous hospitality.

*A letter to the Director General from an Honorary Colonel Commandant*      *January 1994*

What a magnificent event!...

Thank you for your hospitality last night – first class catering and first class company. I am sure that we will all remember it for many years to come.

I hope that the pain killers didn't completely wear off before you got home and that recovery will be speedy. My great admiration for keeping a stiff and even humorous upper lip!

*Letter to Director of Clothing and Textiles from the Chief Executive of Remploy (Sponsors of Corps events).*      *January 1994*

## Livery Companies, Kineton 18 February 1994

I confirm the following attendance:

Master Mr Roy Rutter Boots size 10

1st Warden – Mr Richard Vanderpump – (Own boots)

Past Master – Mr Geoffrey Perkins – Boots size 9

Past Master – Mr Derek Kaye – Boots size 9

Court Assistant – Mr Peter Nathan – Boots size 9

Court Assistant – Mr Brian Jones – Boots size 10

Court Assistant – Mr Keith Kirby – Boots size 9

Court Assistant – Mr Peter Padley-Smith – Boots size 10

Court Assistant – Mr Peter Istead – (Own boots)Clerk

Mr John Williams – Boots size 11

All know that they must be at the School by 0930. As most are travelling from London, I suspect they will in fact `over-insure' and arrive early! I have told them that their names will be known, at the gate, but they may be required to produce some proof of identity. They also have your draft programme of events.

The Master, 1st Warden and Clerk will be robed for the ceremony. Otherwise, I have said "suits and insignia".

You will see (above) that I have obtained boot sizes (for Wellies!). You did say that waterproof jackets can also be provided if weather proves inclement.

*A letter from the Clerk to the Company of Gold and Silver Wyre Drawers*      *January 1994*

**Expedition to India**. It has come to my attention that a team from 3 Tank Transporter Squadron plan to trek in India from 14 February to 31 March 1994.

The Defence Attaché has suggested that this would be an ideal opportunity to cement our alliance with the Indian Army Service Corps and it is also the wish of the

ABOVE: The Colonel-in-Chief visits RLVC *Ardennes* and her crew in Hong Kong on the disbandment of 415 Maritime Troop (Logistic Support Branch HQ British Forces Hong Kong). BELOW: The Land Canoe squad (Supply Services Hong Kong).

Commanding Officer 7 Transport Regiment. Should you agree to this action, the Defence Attaché has asked that you write through him to the Director General Supply and Transport. A draft for the purpose is attached.

*A letter from Regimental Colonel to the Director General* *January 1994*

**Corps Dinner.** My Master, Mr E R Britt JP, has asked me to send you his thanks, to which I add my own, for having so kindly invited us to the excellent Dinner Night at your Corps' Headquarters Mess at Deepcut last Thursday, which we both enjoyed tremendously.It was a great privilege for us to be presented to your Deputy Colonel-in-Chief, HRH The Duke of Gloucester, and we were both greatly impressed with the degree of integration between the various constituents of your Corps, which has been achieved over such a relatively short period.

*A letter to the Director General from the Clerk to the Worshipful Company of Carmen*

*February 1994*

**Painting of Her Royal Highness The Duchess of Kent.** It was gratifying that my portrait of your Deputy Colonel-in–Chief, Her Royal Highness The Duchess of Kent, was so well received, and I hope I have similar success with Her Royal Highness The Princess Royal. I thought the painting looked well hanging on the wall. Please thank John Hambleton for making the necessary arrangements.

*Mara McGregor, Artist.* *February 1994*

**Corps Expenditure**. I felt that I should inform you of two commissions that must be proceeded with now. They are:

**Horses Brasses.** A somewhat arcane subject! Commander Supply London District appeared mounted on parade sporting tack with Corps pattern brasses. We have inherited this tradition and style and `face'

require us to produce new Corps brasses. Every effort will be made to minimise costs but I anticipate the bill will be £3,500 (mainly because of the die costs). Colonel Fisher is due to appear on parade in two months time and I need to crack on if the brasses are to be ready in time.

**Cuneo Cartoon.** Terence Cuneo has agreed to paint a mouse cartoon for us. Some of you may have seen an example in the Mill Hill Mess. The concept is as on the attached sketch. The group of mice on the left will be in old Corps mess kit; that on the right, in General Staff and new mess kit. The cost will be about£2000

Director General Logistic Support (Army) and Director Logistic Support Policy have already given approval in principle for these projects. Trustees have already approved for 1994 £20,000 for historical items and this fund has not been used and can thus easily contain these costs. I would be grateful for any views by 24 February, please.

*A letter from the Regimental Colonel to the Trustees* *February 1994*

**Exchange Appointments**. It was good to talk to you the other day and I would once again like to thank you for the new Corps flag which was sent to me by Mike Procter whilst you were away on duty. This flag was presented to the Headquarters of the United States 3rd Air Force at Mildenhall where it now has pride of place in the office of the Deputy Chief of Staff Logistics, Colonel Keith Ashby, with whom we have a close working relationship and where it will be seen by his many important visitors

*Extract from a letter from Commanding Officer 496 Movement Control Unit RLC(V)* *February 1994*

**Beads for the Natives.** Thank you for your bluey of 27 January 1994 and the request for something RLC for the exiles. Your plea has

ABOVE: Op Gabriel in the Air Mounting Centre (29 Regiment). BELOW:
Motor cycling on ice in Norway (42 Squadron).

touched the heart of this hard-nosed Treasurer and some `bits and pieces' are enclosed. Don't come too often – next time you pay! With best wishes.
*A letter to J2 Logistics (Falklands) from the Regimental Treasurer* February 1994

**Affiliations.** You may be aware that the Malaysian Army Service Corps and the Malaysian Army Ordnance Corps were, respectively, allianced to the Royal Corps of Transport and the Royal Army Ordnance Corps. These alliances date back many years and reflect similar affiliations with Australia, India, Pakistan, New Zealand and Sri Lanka.

The Royal Corps of Transport and the Royal Army Ordnance Corps were amalgamated in April 1993 to form a new Corps, The Royal Logistic Corps, and it is the wish of the old Corps and the new, to carry forward the alliances. The terms of the arrangement are fraternal and entirely pragmatic, so there are no binding commitments.

On our part, we would hope to keep you informed of any important changes to our organisation, send you our Corps Journal for information and offer a point of contact for personnel on courses or otherwise in this country on duty.
*A letter to the Chairman of the Army Ordnance Corps of Malaysia* February 1994

**Corps Coaching Club.** Everybody has been very impressed with the enthusiasm of the Royal Corps of Transport and now The Royal Logistic Corps in getting their coaches back on the road. I don't always feel we have done as much for you as we should have done. I also appreciate the difficulties for the Corps to do this, in times when everybody is so critical of anything out of the ordinary

Please pass my thanks to the Chef for an excellent dinner and his staff for looking after us so well. Looking forward to seeing you during the summer.
*Secretary, The Coaching Club* April 1994

**Association Membership.** I acknowledge receipt today the arrival of the Constitution Rules and Membership Card as a member of the Regimental Association of The Royal Logistic Corps, together with a lapel badge.

I am happy to tell you that I do receive a copy of The Royal Logistic Corps *Journal*, which I find immensely interesting. I must say that I am very impressed with the professional manner, not only of the publication of the Journal, but also with the items mentioned above. Sadly I will not be able to attend The Royal Logistic Corps Corps Saturday, as I have another engagement on that day.

Although my old Service, The Royal Pioneer Corps, holds many memories for me, I am nevertheless very proud indeed to be a member of The Royal Logistic Corps Association. One represents the past and the other the future. Incidently I do possess a RLC non-crease silk tie, which is excellent value for money.

My good wishes to you and your staff for the future.
*Letter from a retired member to the Regimental Secretary.* May 1994

**Tank Transporter Driver Badge.** It is true that presently the Tank Transporter trade badge is worn on a variety of uniforms. This letter is written to explain the reasons for this and to ask that Reference A be amended to reflect what we feel is a proud requirement of today's Tank Transporter trade. You should be aware that the badge is not worn by personnel other than Tank Transporter Drivers and there are no plans to ever issue these badges to non-A Tradesmen.
*Extract from a 7 Transport Regiment letter to the Dress Committee* May 1994

ABOVE: Humanitarian aid for Russia (62 Transport & Movements Squadron, Berlin). BELOW: 79 Railway Squadron and 275 Railway Squadron (V) on annual camp, 1994.

**Sports Calender – May 1994**

2 : RLC Tug of War – Aldershot Horse Show

2-7 : RLC Motor Cycling: Scottish 6 Day Trial – Fort William

4 : RLC RUFC: Army Corps 7-a-side Competition – Aldershot

9 : RLC Unit Sailing: Officers Offshore Sailing Day : Solent

10 : RLC Yacht Club: Commanding Officers Open Day Gosport/Solent/Stokes Bay

11 : RLC Corps Coaching – Royal Windsor Horse Show

12 : RLC Yacht Club Brass Hat Regatta – Netley/Solent

19 : RLC Golf: Spring Meeting – Tidworth

22 : RLC Rowing: Joint Service Regatta – Peterborough

26 : RLC Cricket Club: 1st XI versus Army Medical Services Woolwich

27 : RLC Basketball: RLC UK versus RLC BAOR – Aldershot

*Extract from RLC Sports Calender.* *May 1994*

**Meeting of the Colonels Commandant.** Major General Botting reported that he and Colonel Barnett had begun their tenures with a busy programme of visits. He noted that their impressions were entirely encouraging and that newly formed units were quickly becoming integrated with local communities.

He and the outgoing Representative had had audiences with the Royal Colonels and in each case were pleased to hear that the Corps style of presentation was well received and that there was evident interest in the Corps and enthusiasm for involvement with Corps affairs.

He also attended Founders Day and noted that Major General Carrington had visited In Pensioners. There was some discussion about sponsorship of Chelsea Pensioners by units of the Corps and the Regimental Colonel was directed to liaise with Forming Corps and the Chelsea Hospital to discuss liaison. Afternote: This is in hand and a report on progress will be given at the next meeting.)

*Extracts from the Representative Colonel Commandant and the Director General's reports* *June 1994*

**Carrier Pigeons.** I am writing to ask information (photography, documents, bibliography) about the subject *The utilization of carrier pigeons in the World War One.* I am working in research work into Spanish specialized ilustrated paper I know that the English Army use of double-decker bus for to be able to take many pigeons to the Front trench.

All the information that you issue, I shall return together with a free copy where it will publicized the article.

Thank you very much for all.

*A letter from Madrid* *June 1994*

**Corps Dinner.** I thought your new batch of officers first rate and I was very interested to talk to them. They were all very articulate and enthusiastic. We are very fortunate to have such quality.

*A letter to the Director General from the Chief of the General Staff* *June 1994*

The Chief of the General Staff was asking me about our training and motivation methods and seemed genuinely interested in The Unipart `U'. He expressed an interest in visiting us to learn more about it. We would, of course, be delighted to have him do so, accompanied by yourself if you feel that to be appropriate.

May I also say how impressed I was by the calibre of your team. We have room in Unipart for such as they

*A letter to the Director General from Managing Director Unipart (sponsors of Corps Rugby) to the Director General* *June 1994*

**D-Day Landings, Arromanches 1944: Letters.** Following a very necessary days rest and relaxation, I feel better able to express my thanks for the honour of being included in the Normandy safari.

ABOVE: Lance Corporal Ruddon, Staff Sergeant Robey and Lance Corporal Witt at the 1994 Royal Tournament (Postal & Courier Services).
BELOW: A Commander tank transporter prime mover at the Worshipful Company of Carmen's Annual Cart Marking Ceremony, Guildhall, London, 1993.

No doubt better pens than mine will adequately express the appreciation of the programming and effort involved by you and your entire team to achieve, so successfully, a truly memorable trip.

One has memories of June 1944 – now one has vastly more pleasant memories of June 1994. Thank you one and all – it will never be forgotten.

Firstly, I would like to thank you and The Royal Logistic Corps for inviting me to join the party to commemorate the D–Day Landing and to be present at the unveiling of the memorial plaque at Arromanches – it was a very impressive and emotional occasion.

Although I didn't land from the LCL until mid-day D+3 it brought back vivid memories of wading ashore, not knowing what to expect, and then moving up through the Arromanches gap to join the main body of my unit. I thought the BBC TV coverage on the Monday struck the right mood of the occasion.

The arrangements you made for our visit were first class – many thanks.

*From a retired Forming Corps officer who accompanied the Corps team to the unveiling of a commemorative plaque at Arromanches to our predecessors*      *June 1994*

**Motor Cycling.** You will recall that Reference A addressed the subject of two bids for capital which were recommended by the Central Sports Committee in principle but which were beyond the budget of that committee. You approved the bid for further expenditure on parachuting and awaited a recommendation from the President of Motor Cycling before agreeing to further expenditure on Motor Cycling; this latter bid has now been received.

The attached report demonstrates both the success of Motor Cycling at Army and national level and the existing financial commitment of those who are currently competing. This increase can be coped with within the anticipated 1995 Budget.

*A Regimental Headquarters letter to Trustees. July 1994*

**Not that Sporting.** Though still maintaining a reasonable general interest in sport, as a veteran World War Two type (in 1945 active in Germany with an ad hoc 2nd Army Troops Sports Committee), please *refrain from forwarding any further issues* of "Sporting Journal".

Of course, I may be mistaken, but I consider this an unnecessary, expensive and quite obviously an excessively time consuming exercise.

*From a retired Association member*      *July 1994*

**Corps Weekend Silver Display.** Welcome to the Headquarters Officers' Mess of The Royal Logistic Corps. The building was formerly the Headquarters Mess of the Royal Army Ordnance Corps and was opened in 1974 by General Sir William Jackson. It became The Royal Logistic Corps Headquarters Mess on the formation of The Royal Logistic Corps on 5 April 1993 from the Royal Corps of Transport, Royal Army Ordnance Corps, Royal Pioneer Corps, Army Catering Corps and Postal and Courier Services (Royal Engineers).

The display you see today is based on the furniture and silver owned by the Forming Corps and loaned to The Royal Logistic Corps. We have since added items of our own to complete the display. All the items you see are privately owned and funded by officers' subscriptions to the Mess of a half Day's Pay each year.

The display is based on two dining room tables set for dinner and a separate silver display. For today we have used the ante-room, with its many portraits as a backcloth to the display.

*Extract from the pamphlet on the opening to the public of the Headquarters Officers' Mess on the Corps at home*

*July 1994*

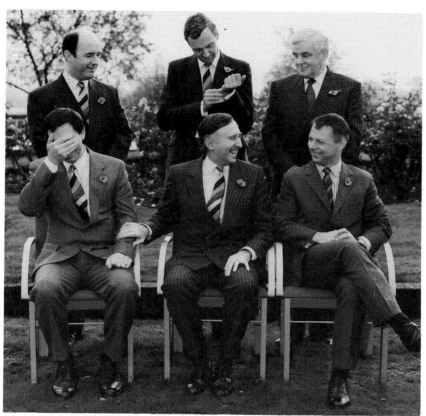

ABOVE: Staff of PB10, 1994. Rear: Majors G A O'Sullivan and M R Lilley and Lieutenant Colonel (Retired) A Young. Front: Major M R Lanham, Colonel N E L Gilbert and Major P F Stamps. BELOW: Vessels of 17 Port & Maritime Regiment form the backdrop to the 50th Anniversary of D-Day Commemorative Parade at Arromanches, 6 June 1994. (Courtesy of Mr Brian Smith of *The Daily Telegraph*)

### First Corps Sunday
### The Lesson
### Read by Major General D L Burden CBE
### Director General
### The Collect of
### The Royal Logistic Corps

All:

God our Father, whose Son Jesus Christ ministered to the needs of mankind, may we of The Royal Logistic Corps, so tackle the diverse tasks assigned to us, that wherever we serve, on land or sea or in the air we may sustain our comrades both in peace and war, and thus be found worthy of those whom we seek to support, for the sake of Jesus Christ our Lord. Amen.

*Dedication of the Formation Memorial Plaque*
*Extract from the Order of Service for the first*
*Corps Sunday*                              *4 July 1994*

**Lanyard – Correct Method of Attachment**. It is requested that the dress regulations (Reference A and B) pertaining to the wearing of The Royal Logistic Corps Lanyards are confirmed. It would appear to be practice in many areas, including amongst some senior officers of the Corps, to wear the lanyard hanging outside the pocket, attached using the whistle clip, to the right or left of the centre button of the left pocket. Reference A however states that the end should directly enter the left pocket on the left side.

Clarification is required and should be promulgated, including a tactful indication to senior officers of the correct method of lanyard attachment. Perhaps the best available example of this confusion is seen in Corps Journal photographs, where the methods of attachment appear equally divided.

*A tactful letter from the Staff.*          *July 1994*

**Skinners Horse Table.** Skinners Horse (1st Duke of York's Own Cavalry) was formed in 1803 and then commanded by James Skinner. In 1922, the 2nd Regiment was disbanded and the table was brought to the United Kingdom by General Sir Richard Ewart who presented it to the Royal Army Service Corps Mess in Buller Barracks in 1926.

**The Cairo Table.** The Cairo table is a pre-war table used for the Allied Conference at Mena House, Cairo in November and December 1943 for the meeting between President Roosevelt, Prime Minister Winston Churchill, President Inono of Turkey and Marshal and Mrs Chang Kai Chek. There is a silver plate set into the table to commemorate visits to the mess by Her Majesty The Queen in her capacity as Colonel-in-Chief of the Royal Army Ordnance Corps.

The table is laid for dinner using Royal Logistic Corps table mats, crockery and cutlery and silver goblets presented over the period 1887 to 1987. The major centre pieces are:

Candelabra – Silver plate dating from 1950 and presented to Army Catering Corps by the Royal Corps of Transport in 1965

GS Wagon – Silver dated 1965 and presented to the Royal Army Ordnance Corps by the Royal Corps of Transport in 1965. Based on a GS Wagon owned by the Royal Corps of Transport.

St Barbara – Silver dated 1993 and presented to The Royal Logistic Corps by the Royal Army Ordnance Corps on formation.

Thunderbird – Silver dated 1956. Serviced by 7 Guided Missile Company Royal Army Ordnance Corps.

Statuette – Silver dated 1956. A model of an airborne soldier.

Statuette – Silver dated 1985, to commemorate the disbandment of the Royal Army Ordnance Corps Apprentices' College.

*Extracts from the pamphlet on the opening to the public of the Headquarters Officers' Mess on the Corps at home.*          *July 1994*

ABOVE: Pipes and Drums of the Scottish Transport Regiment (V).
BELOW: 150 (Yorkshire) Transport Regiment (V) stops the traffic in the
city centre during the Freedom of Hull Parade, 1994.

**The Saga of the Hat.** In March 1993, amidst a flurry of great excitement prior to the amalgamation of my former Corps, the Army Catering Corps, into The Royal Logistic Corps, I ordered my RLC No 1 Dress Field Officer's Hat from a company of great repute (allegedly) and recommended by RLC Regimental Headquarters (and who were we to argue with the RHQ).

I sent a cheque for some £65.00 which was cashed not long after and to date, only a year and three months later, I have received nothing.

Being a patient caterer, I waited until the new year and in January 1994 I rang the Company and spoke to a gentleman, who I can only assume uses the name of manager who, almost beside himself with apologies, promised to send the hat that very afternoon.

Two weeks later and now into February, I rang again and asked where my hat was. "Have you not received it yet?" was the reply. "No", was the answer, and after I had spelt out my unit address here in Germany phonetically the `Manager', yet again full of regret and apologies, promised to put the hat in the post.

In March I rang him again and asked where my hat was. He promised to send it in the post and as a gesture of his sincerity (ha ha) he asked me for the Logistic Support Branch fax number so he could fax me a copy of the parcel serial number.

Funnily enough I rang him again in April 1994 and asked him where my hat was. This time he used the Red Star parcel ploy and said he would fax me the Red Star parcel number: could he have the fax number. I informed him that the fax number was the same as the one I gave him last month and would he use it this time and send the hat.

Well, well, I rang him again in May and asked where my hat was. "Have you not received it yet?" was the unexpected reply. "We have just received a delivery of field officers' peaks and have almost completed your hat and will send it off today." Not usually stuck for words I thanked him and put the phone down. I then wrote to my solicitor to ask for some advice. My solicitor informs me that for the trifling sum of some £65 worth of hat the costs of legal action would re-equip my entire wardrobe.

I rang him again in the middle of June and asked where my hat was. "It was sent on the 6th of June" was the reply. "Isn't that extraordinary", I said, "I haven't received it. Could it be that you haven't sent it? Please do so." Once again full of apology he agreed to send the hat and later on in the day rang me to give me a parcel number. I can now only assume it was a number read off the side of a box or whatever!

In a sort of perverse way I find this all rather amusing and am incapable of anger. I rang him this very morning. "It was sent on the 28th of June", was the reply. "This being the case", says I, "I should have some five or six Royal Logistic Corps No 1 Dress Field Officer hats in my possession and yet I have none." He even read a parcel number to me and has agreed to fax it yet again.

*Now why don't I believe him. Over to you*
*A letter from a cross officer.*                    *July 1994*


**Officer Recruiting.** Without a doubt, this lady has tried her best throughout the course. Despite being enthusiastic towards an Army career, she simply failed to project her lovely personality on the group and influence their actions in any way. During the outdoor tasks phase she was content to be led rather than lead. Her lack of practical ideas meant her plan was sketchy and soon the other, stronger members took over her task. Unfortunately, she is naturally very quietly spoken and this meant she was difficult to hear – both in the discussion phases and her own lecturette. In summary despite her enthusiasm, she should be discouraged from attending the Regular Commissions Board without damaging her confidence.
*Corps Recruiting & Liaison Officer report on a*
*female potential officer candidate at pre-RCB*
*August 1994.*

ABOVE: Warrant Office One (Regimental Sergeant Major) V E Mahan BEM taking his annual bath on Battle Camp 93 (55 MC Squadron, 29 Regiment. LEFT: Gurkha Gladiators in Kathmandu (British Gurkhas Nepal); RIGHT: The OC 'in action' (21 Squadron, 3 Close Support Regiment).

**Double Dutch Enquiries.** I got your address from the Airborne museum in OOSTERBEEK near ARNHEM in The Netherlands and the Airborne Forces Museum in ALDERSHOT. I asked the people at OOSTERBEEK something about the Royal Army Service Corps during the Second World War and so they gave me your address. Why do I like to know something of the Royal Army Service Corps? During the festivity and commeratives around Market Garden there was a large collone of vehicles "CORRIDOR" driving the same as during the days of market garden, I watch that fantastic side, I had a cap from the D-day museum in Portsmouth wich I clipped the insigne of RASC during that periode, there was a english soldier asking me where I got that insigne from I told I got it from my Grand-father. He got it from a soldier who was staying during that time periode in my home-town of Helmond, so I got interrested in this

The english soldier told me that it was a very rare insigne and that the name was change to Royal Corps of Logistics. The reason I send you this letter is this. Is there any information or books about the RASC, what kind of corps was the RASC, and are there any information where they stayed and at what time period that stayed in the region of Helmond during september 17th and the end of the year 1944.

A guy of the Airborne museum at OOSTERBEEK near ARNHEM told me there will be a book shortly comming out about the RASC. Where can I get this book? I visited in july of 1994 in Portsmouth the D-day museum and the South-wick house "HMS Draiden", that was really fantastic? Looking forward to your answer,

*A member of the public in The Netherlands*

**Warrant Officers Class One Convention.** May I thank you for the excellent convention last week. The organisation and presentations were "eye openers" and informative. With regard to the proposed Charter for the Central Mess, none of my Mess members was in favour at all of the contribution to a central Mess even after explaining in full the advantages!

On a brighter note that yellow tie is bloody awful. Jez, if you can think of any way to perhaps redress this I would be more than willing to promote it in a perhaps different light.

*A letter to the Regimental Warrant Officer from a Regimental Sergeant Major.*        *October 1994*

**Headquarters Sergeants' Mess Tie.** After having time to read through the Charter for The Royal Logistic Corps Central Sergeants' Mess tie, which of course, will be talked about for many years to come, I look forward to introducing this to my Mess!! I will pass on any comments made.

*Letter to the Regimental Warrant Officer from a Regimental Sergeant Major of a Territorial Army Regiment.*        *October 1994*

I bet you're glad the Convention is behind you for this year.

With regards to the Sergeants Mess tie I think the yellow one must have our vote – who's going to argue with the Special Air Service anyway?!

*Letter from a Staff Assistant Headquarters Quartermaster General to the Regimental Warrant Officer.*        *October 1994*

**Band Accoutrements.** Further to your fax dated 6 October 1994, concerning Royal Logistic Corps Waist Belts Gold Lace, we regret to inform you that we have drawn a blank with our suppliers of Gold Lace.

We regret therefore that we are unable to offer our quotation against the specification supplied. If however you are able to supply the lace please contact us again.

*A letter from a Tailor*        *October 1994*

LEFT: A Regimental Mouse by Terence Cuneo. (Courtesy of the owner)
RIGHT: Corporal Sutton and his team on the streets of Northern Ireland
(12 Squadron, Moscow Camp). BELOW: Corporal Stott floating his
bundle on exercise (9 Supply Regiment).

**The Carmen Sword Award**. Director General Logistic Support (Army) has seen the submission submitted for The Carmen Sword. Without prompting he came to the same conclusion as you.

Will you now promulgate to all who submitted with a suitable comment to the effect that all were very worthy contenders and let the Clerk to the Worshipful Company of Carmen know.

*Letter from Director Logistic Support Policy regarding the winner of the Carmen Sword for The Most Promising Young Officer.*     *October 1994*

**St Dunstan's Charity**. I am writing on behalf of the St Dunstan's Summer Camp committee to thank you for your most generous contribution to the cost of running the 50th anniversary camp.

The camp was a great success and the anniversary was celebrated in style on the Thursday. In the afternoon the St Dunstaners were driven in a convoy of Aston Martins to the Portsmouth D-Day Museum and in the evening an anniversary dinner was held in the Wardroom, HMS *Daedalus*, with Admiral of the Fleet Sir Henry Leach, the Chairman of St Dunstan's, as the guest of honour.

*A letter to the Regimental Headquarters from the Hampshire Secretary of St Dunstan's October 1994*

**Hand Embroidered Badges/Regalia**. We would like to draw your kind attention to your letter RHQ 39 dated 20 January 1994.

We hope you would be in need of badges now and we are confident that you will definitely favour us with your valued order along with sample. We assure you of our best services at all the times.

Thanking you and look forward to hear from you soon.

With best regards.

*Letter from a Company in Pakistan.*

*November 1994*

**Award of Colours**. 1. The award of Corps Colours is to be assessed in the first instance by the individual sports, and recommended by the Sports President. These recommendations should be raised on 1st April for winter sports and 1 October for summer sports and sent to RHQ The Royal Logistic Corps.

2. The Regimental Colonel is empowered to approve the award of Corps Colours in the name of the Chairman of the Central Sports Committee and is to record each award. Ties, silk squares and badges are issued at regimental expense.

3. In assessing the award of Corps Colours, Sports officials should take into account:

a. Corps Colours should be awarded only after frequent representation of the Corps at a standard above that of the balance of other team or squad members.

b. A single selection at Army, Combined Service or National level would normally attract the award of Corps Colours.

c. Long serving officials with a suitable degree of competence within a particular sport, may be awarded Corps Colours for the administration of that sport.

d. Commanders may need to identify sporting excellence for sports which do not have a formal Corps structure.

4. Advice on all Corps Colours matters can be sought from the Regimental Secretary.

*An extract from the Corps Instruction on Sport*
*November 1994*

**Talavera County School, Aldershot**. Thank you for the cheque for £69.95 which I received in the post this morning. I would also like to take this opportunity of thanking all those members of The Royal Logistic Corps, on behalf of the school, for their generosity in sponsoring the cost of the Polaroid camera.

There are numerous occasions in the life and work of a school when an immediate, instant record is needed. The camera will allow us to do this. We have always valued the connection between The Royal Logistic

ABOVE: Not the most comfortable experience (33 Supply Squadron, 4 General Support Regiment). BELOW: South Atlantic Catering staff at RAF Mount Pleasant, Falkland Islands, 1994.

Corps and our school, and wish to maintain this association in a close and meaningful way. Many thanks once again and, if it is not too early, please pass on the school's Christmas greetings to one and all.
*A letter to the Regimental Headquarters from the Headmaster.* *November 1994*

## Sport – Territorial Army.

Progress on Royal Logistic Corps Territorial Army representative sport teams has been slow but positive. A Territorial Army golf side played the Corps in May (only losing narrowly) and it is planned to make this an annual fixture. Also, following a very successful 6-a-side soccer competition in September (also now to be an annual event), a Royal Logistic Corps Territorial Army soccer squad has been formed. A series of fixtures have been arranged for the New Year and there would have been a game against The Royal Logistic Corps team last month if the Corps had not cancelled.

And finally, in order to guarantee the continuation of Exercise Knees Bend (the sponsored ski-ing event held in Scotland for both Regulars and Territorial Army, from February to April each year), 5 Territorial Army Training Regiment at Grantham will now provide the permanent staff and administrative support.
*Extract from the Colonel of Volunteers Report*
*November 1994*

## Corps Dinner – 200th Anniversary of The Royal Waggoners

The Princess Royal has asked me to write and thank you so much for an extremely good dinner last Wednesday in celebration of the formation of the Royal Waggoners 200 years ago.

Her Royal Highness hopes that the assembled company enjoyed the dinner as much as she did and was thrilled to be given the opportunity of meeting so many members, past and present of the Transport Corps.

Finally, I am to say how much Her Royal Highness enjoyed listening to your very interesting speech on this special evening at The Princess Royal Barracks Blackdown
*Lady in Waiting to Her Royal Highness The Princess Royal.* *November 1994*

Congratulations on a very successful commemorative dinner. It was a very enjoyable evening especially the opportunity to see so many old friends. It's also nice to see the Corps recognising the important anniversary inherited from the constituent Corps.
*A letter to the Director General from a past Colonel Commandant.* *November 1994*

The Royal Logistic Corps has come a long way since those early arguments over the Logistic Support Review. There are still some people more concerned with the preservation of the past than the construction of the future but occasions such as that celebratory dinner do an enormous amount to strengthen the position of The Royal Logistic Corps. We respected the traditions of the past, celebrated a chapter in the history of the Corps and demonstrated that The Royal Logistic Corps proudly represents our heritage.
*A letter to the Director General from a recently retired Brigadier.* *November 1994*

Have you had time to draw breath yet? What a truly exciting evening last Wednesday was! Certainly it will live in my memory for a very long time, believe me! I understand from John Hodges' secretary that it is still one of his main topics of conversation too!
*Director Public Sector Operations, Ryder Truck Rental Ltd (sponsor of The Corps Coaching Club)* *November 1994*

## Hong Kong Visit.

I attended HRH The Duchess of Kent on her recent visit to Hong Kong and took the opportunity to pay calls on our staff and units in the Colony. I also spoke to Commander British Forces. The main points I carried away are summarised below.

ABOVE: HRH The Duke of Gloucester visits 5 TA Training Regiment at Grantham on the day of the Lamb Trophy, 1993. BELOW: TA Charity Bike Ride from Edinburgh to Grantham, 1994 (142 Vehicle Squadron (V)). (Courtesy of Sid Barker, Tonbridge)

*HRH Visit.* This went well and there was a well-conceived display and briefing by Lt Col Clough, followed by a reception with officers and senior ranks and their wives. It went down well with those present and I think she enjoyed the visit. HRH observed on the key role played by the Corps in drawdown and on the sensitive way in which local redundancy is being handled. Following this visit she went to Stone Cutters to visit the Hong Kong Military Service Corps in her role as patron of the HKMSC Trust.

Staff Visit Commander Logistic Support. Jonathan Clough and I discussed a number of matters summarised below:

*Corps Memorabilia* I am convinced that we should mark 1997 appropriately. We discussed silver and other options and agreed finally that a significant painting would be most fitting. I recommend that we commission a known and reliable artist to visit in November 1995 (for weather reasons) and to paint probably two scenes: one portraying the Hong Kong soldiers and contemporary uniform; the second a scene of Hong Kong island and the harbour. The administrative costs can be kept low and I estimate that a budget of £15,000 will cover the project. This is comparable to commissioning a relatively modest piece of silver and the result would be infinitely more useful and dramatic. I will recommend including this project in the 1996 financial year budget.

*Final Event.* The Corps residual staff and regiment will want to hold a final event, probably in the spring of 1997, assuming the current drawdown date is held to. The timing and style will have to be left to Hong Kong but I propose putting £2.500 into the budget for 1996 for the purpose.

*Final Band Visit.* I am keen to get the Corps Staff Band out to Hong Kong, possibly to coincide with our own final event. I believe Commander British Forces would welcome as many bands as possible in 1996 and 1997 to

retain a profile. I will ask Commander Logistic Support to ferret at his end but I will need some provisional ideas as soon as possible to pre-empt Kneller Hall. I believe we have a strong morale case but unless we take the high ground we will not get a sniff!

*Other Discussions* I spoke to Commander British Forces briefly and he was highly complimentary of the Corps and keen on the idea of a band visit.

*December 1994 Regimental Colonel's brief to Director General*

**Another Dutch Letter.** Thank you for the information that I go about the RASC during WWII in the southern part of the Netherlands. What you told me about the 21 Army group, did astonish me because i've read some books about 21 army group and i noticed that this was commanded by Field-Marshal Montgomery. I saw in a Book a picture that Montgomery and Eisenhower met in Helmond.

I've read a book that the reason they met in Helmond is, that some General Dempsey got his Headquarters in Helmond, during that period sept. 1944 and 1945. Now these are my questions? Who know's something about this General Dempsey and What was the reason of his stay in then a small town like Helmond, because Eindhoven is a bigger city during WWII. You told me about those 12 lines of communications, what do you mean about this? Looking forward to your answer.

*Part of protracted correspondence with a member of the public in The Netherlands.     December 1994*

**Anthony Nolan National Bike Ride.** You will rue the day we re-met at Sunningdale! I am asking whether we could start our 1995 National Bike Ride at Dalton Barracks, Abingdon on Sunday 25 June. I anticipate that we will have between 1,000 and 2,000 riders and that they will largely come by car. The main requirements are an enormous car park area. If we could pitch a couple of marquees

ABOVE: Corps tennis championships 1994: winners and their trophies.
BELOW: A Corps Select Cricket XI which was victorious against the
Honourable Artillery Company at Deepcut on 2 July 1993.

to provide cover and refreshment areas, it would be marvellous, but, other than that, we would be largely self-sufficient. We would have marshalls and I would not anticipate the Anthony Nolan riders being a burden on the regiment. If you were able to persuade the Commanding Officer to allow us in, it would be simply marvellous because Abingdon is the ideal place for our Thames Valley Ride.
*Letter from the Chief Executive of the Anthony Nolan Trust.* December 1994

**The Mouse Cartoon by Terence Cuneo.** A Mess Night, in the form of a mouse warming party for Her Majesty's newly formed Corps (The Rodent Logistic Corps) just returned from their first exercise on the Cheddar Flats and Caerphilly Foothills, whilst from above the mantle shelf, the portrait of their revered Rodent General, Sir Guzzlington Gruyere OGM* gazes sternly down on the members of his beloved Corps.

*Order of the Golden Mousetrap.

**Note.** Officers dining are dressed in a variety of Mess Kits depicting three RLC Officers (Regimental Colonel, Director Logistic Support (Army) and Director Logistic Support Policy (Army)) as well as representatives of the Forming Corps. (This picture, with the above wording, was used by Terence Cuneo for his 1994 Christmas card.)

**Sports Policy.** The first problem is player availability. Our Corps policy on this matter is quite clear. Selection for a Corps team is not an invitation and it should be treated with the same degree of gravity as any other order or instruction. I know of a number of cases where hard-pressed Secretaries are often struggling to finalise teams and where Corps performance has suffered from late cancellations or from plain and simple failure to appear. Can you all please use your influence to get the message across and follow up when appropriate.
*Extract from a RHQ letter to Sports Presidents* January 1995

**Yachting.** On behalf of my fellow Flag Officers and Members, I send you Greetings from The Royal Bermuda Yacht Club.

1994 was our Sesquicentennial Year and we had many celebrations, including the visit of Her Majesty The Queen and Prince Philip on March 9th; a Gala Ball at Government House on October 1st; and the re-enactment of the 1844 Founding of the Club on October 30th attended by Lord John Kerr, a close relative of our founding Commodore Lord Mark Kerr. There were also other great sailing and non-sailing events throughout the year which rounded out an incredibly successful Sesquicentennial including the 39th Newport to Bermuda Race in June, with an amazing coincidence of 150 yachts on the start line.

Now that our Club has completed this momentous year, we are also upgrading our collection of Burgees from around the world. Sadly, Bermuda's humid climate means that they do not last as long as we would like! This letter asks if you would be so kind as to send us one of your burgees for display in the Club. I look forward to hearing that we have been successful in our request.
*A letter to the Regimental Colonel from the Commodore The Royal Bermuda Yacht Club* January 1995

**Corps Dinner.** Thank you for forwarding me the photograph to mark the occasion of the Commemorative Dinner held at Deepcut on 2 November 1994. The photograph is a wonderful memento of a most illustrious occasion and brings back many happy memories.
*Letter to the Regimental Warrant Officer from the past Quartermaster General* January 1995

**Headquarters Sergeants' Mess – Dinner Night.** I would like to personally thank and congratulate you for planning and executing such a prestigious Corps dinner night on Tuesday.

ABOVE: Mill Hill Post Office (BFPO 777), 1994. BELOW: The Mouse
Cartoon by Terence Cuneo.

The Scottish Transport Regiment personnel who attended had a super evening and thoroughly enjoyed renewing old acquaintances. I am positive that His Royal Highness could not fail to be impressed by the spirit, open friendliness and camaraderie displayed by everyone associated with the Corps Mess.

It was a pleasure to have been a part of such a great evening and I believe it to be the catalyst from which many more successful Corps events will emerge. Please pass on my thanks to all the mess staff for providing us with such professional standards of layout and cuisine, their attention to detail was admirable. I look forward to seeing you in the near future.

*A letter from the Regimental Sergeant Major of the Scottish Transport Regiment to the Regimental Warrant Officer on the Dining In of His Royal Highness The Duke of Gloucester* January 1995

**Unveiling of Colonel-in-Chief's Portrait.** Thank you so very much for the wonderful reception and luncheon which you arranged for the unveiling of the portrait of Her Royal Highness, Princess Anne, on Wednesday.

The lunch was simply delicious, and how lovely to eat to that soft music. It was good to see you again and so meet once again old acquaintances. What fun it all was and we look forward to seeing you at the Duke of Gloucester unveiling in due course!

*Mara McGregor, painter of Her Royal Highness The Princess Royal His Royal Highness The Duke of Gloucester Her Royal Highness The Duchess of Kent* January 1995

**Ties and Scarves.** As one now in the upper sixties and who in cold weather wears a wool scarf I write to enquire whether there would be any possibility of the Association members – subject, of course to the matter being discussed by the Council – being able to purchase a scarf to match the excellent ties which have been produced.

The scarf of the Palestine Police Old Comrades Association is a full length wool scarf in black, white and russet (not dissimilar to the London University convocation colours!) and I feel that a scarf would make a useful sartorial addition to our wardrobe and perhaps a nice scarf/headscarf for the ladies?

Over to you!

*Letter from a Retired Association Member* January 1995

**Corps Dinner.** I should like to express my thanks to yourself and to the Corps for the hospitality extended to me last evening at your Corps Dinner night. The food, wine and good company in a delightful setting – were enjoyed immensely. It was nice to renew acquaintances and particularly interesting to meet various catering and catering support personnel of RLC.

If you have the opportunity please pass on my regards to Brigadier Andrew Fisher and my thanks for 'looking after me' during the evening and for 'seeing me home'.

Many thanks for a splendid evening.

*From the Master of The Worshipful Company of Cooks* January 1995

**Officer Recruiting.** I write to you following a rather unfortunate incident at my Medical Board on 9 December 1994 – I failed! As a result of this, I received a stock letter from DAR1b (Candidates Section) thanking me for my application but regretting that I could not be considered further. I am sure that this is not news to you, as you obviously take a keen interest in all your potential officers' fortunes. What you may not be aware of is the reason for my failure, so at the risk of turning your stomach, I shall elucidate. At age eight I underwent surgery to lower an undescended testicle.

*Letter from a potential officer candidate.*

January 1995

ABOVE: Warrant Officer One Jones, National Chef of 1994, is congratulated by his wife. (Photo courtesy of PRG Publicity, Eastbourne) BELOW: The Culinary World Cup team in St Omer Barracks (Army School of Catering).

**Regimental Association.** Maybe a little surprised you can – and have bothered to – identify the over 80s. Will you please convey to those Trustees my appreciations for the thought contained within your very kind letter of the 12 January. It really is nice to be remembered.

Having regard to the general ups and downs of life and particularly insofar as World War 2 years are concerned I am myself astounded to reach 80!

By the way it delights me to see how you sign off.

Very happily I'll repeat it.Yours aye.
*A letter from a retired Association member*
*January 1995*

**On granting free Journals to Association members over 80 years old.** I am sorry not to have replied before now to your very welcome letter of 12 January, awarding me the prize, having reached the age of 80, of receiving The Royal Logistic Corps Journal free for the rest of my life.

This is very kind; in return may I suggest that instead the £10.00 pa should continue to be paid into whatever fund may be useful to you. If this involves any paperwork, please send it to me.

With all good wishes and thanks for the excellent work you are doing
*A letter from a retired Association Member*
*February 1995*

**The Corps of Drums – Guildhall Dinner.** You must have been very proud last night of your Corps of Drums since they were without doubt the highlight of the entire evening.

I would like to ask you to pass on my thanks to all concerned. I am sure your Colonel in Chief was as impressed as the remainder of the great hall.

Thank you once again.
*A letter to Regimental Colonel after a performance attended by the Colonel-in-Chief and The Prime Minister*
*February 1995*

**The Journal Coming.** Please keep the Journal coming through my door – it is an excellent read and my wife and I spend hours searching through to read of the exploits of old friends, as well as searching for the winners of our `not plain English award'. February's winner, by a mile, was 24 Transport and Movement Regiment – what was that last paragraph all about?! Well done in mastering the Desk Top Publisher – keep up the good work.
*A letter from the British Military Mission, Kuwait*
*February 1995*

**Exchange Posts.** I am due to end my tour in the Pentagon in August or September of this year. I will ensure that my successor receives a fair proportion (one third or one quarter) of the grant upon my departure from this appointment.

'Who is the happy Warrior? Who is he
That every man in arms should wish to be?
Pour, varlet, pour the water,
The water steaming hot!
A spoonful for each man of us,
Another for the pot.'

Happy to have served in this outstanding appointment, but equally happy to be returning to the 'green and promised land', where people know how to brew a real pot of tea!

Please pass my thanks to the Sub-Committee for enabling me to `promote' our Corps during my tour in the United States
*A letter from the British Liaison Officer, The Pentagon, Washington DC*  *February 1995*

**Regimental Lunch.** Thank you so much – all of you in Regimental Headquarters – for inviting me to your very pleasant lunch party yesterday. The meal was delicious and I met some very interesting people, including of course Bernard Kashket whom I had not seen for a year or two and who is now full of his Royal Warrant!

ABOVE: Cyclists of the AMF (L) Supply Squadron relaxing in Monte Carlo, 1993. BELOW: Postal & Courier Depot, Mill Hill, winners of the hockey Bari Bowl, 1993.

It was kind of you to invite me. My only comment is that by my standards I have not been able to do enough for you to warrant such generosity. I look forward to sorting out with you ways in which I can sing (or write) for my (supper) lunch more effectively!
*A letter to Regimental Colonel from the Secretary of the Army Museums Ogilby Trust*
*February 1995*

**Ladies Mess Kit.** Thank you very much for delivering my mess kit on time. I was able to wear it and it was much admired, however, as I am now returning it you will gather that, although it is wearable, it is not right. Considering the cost of the uniform I am sure that you will not be surprised that we are going to persevere until it is perfect!
*An extract from a letter to a Tailor   February 1995*

***Scite, Cito, Certe.*** The motto of the Worshipful Company of Carmen (in the City of London) means skillfully, swiftly, surely — and that epitomises 'the change'. Twenty years ago the then RCT teamed up with the Carmen in a formal association — some of us, with shades of post-war National Service, were a little hesitant about being swamped by what we wrongly perceived as the incoming Colonel Blimp. As we soon found out, there were also plenty of soldiers who wondered about those City folk, with crystallised rules, crusted port and even crustier attitudes. Both views soon changed.

When we celebrated the first decade, as the then Master I was already a total convert to a close and affectionate liaison, privileged to be an honorary soldier and a vocal support force whenever army or Corps were called in question. Then Options for Change threatened our useful love affair. How would we find the cooks and postmen, the ammo wallahs and the earthmovers? And what about the other two City Guilds with similar associations with Forming Corps?

We should have known better. Forming Corps soldiery came, saw and conquered us.

In their wisdom, the powers envisaged a continuing romance, and new Articles of Association were promulgated. The Carmen's Sword of Honour is still our annual pleasure, 25 Freight Squadron RLC still 'The Carmen's Own', and we still seek annual candidates for the RLC Safety Award, while dining the Corps each April, and maintaining a seat for the valued Honorary Assistant Director General and our Corps Liaison Officer in our counsels. It is as if nothing's changed, yet on a wider, better canvas.

Mind you, my first visit to Deepcut was a revelation — where were the medals? What were those paintings? And who on earth parades on those endless squares? God's Acre is a loss, but once the fencing's screened, there'll be a better view from RHQ. The only trouble's finding it. Do Ordnance like to hide? It was a friendly lady soldier with a formidable piece of hardware who finally rescued me from the backwoods, down a one-way winding lane, far from John Hambleton's anxious eye, and pointed the errors of my way.

Now the medals are safely ensconced, the Mess welcoming, the Corps of Drums survived, the whole military and regimental panoply retailored, without late delivery, missing insignia or ill-fitting kit. One can truly say the Forming Corps, like all good friends who've reached their end-game, are gone, while greatly revered, but not forgotten, so long live the new Corps and, in our own Carmen's immortal phrase, 'Long may it continue and flourish forever'.
*Past Master Clive Birch,*
*Carmen's Company*

### SENIOR APPOINTMENTS
**Senior officers of the Corps occupied the following appointments as at 31 January 1995:**
Major General D L Burden CBE
*Director General Logistic Support (Army)*
Major General M S White CBE
*Director Support Headquarters Allied Land Forces Central Europe*
Brigadier T Dalby-Welsh

ABOVE: On the obstacle course. It's easy when you know how (35 Squadron, 3 Close Support Regiment). BELOW: Commando Ordnance Squadron at the Spean Bridge Commando Memorial, 1993.

*Director Material Supply and Distribution (Army)*
Brigadier R N Lennox CBE
*Director Land Service Ammunition*
Brigadier R F Mendham GM
*Director General Information Technology Systems*
Brigadier N Muddiman CBE
*Commandant Army School of Mechanical Transport*
Brigadier I N Osborne
*Director Discipline*
Brigadier A W Lyons CBE
*Student Royal College of Defence Studies*
Brigadier G A Ewer CBE
*Director Logistic Operations (Army)*
Brigadier R H T Kirby CBE
*Director Defence Clothing and Textiles Authority*
Brigadier A Fisher
*Director of Catering (Army)*
Brigadier P A Flanagan
*Commander Logistic Support Headquarters United Kingdom Land Forces*
Brigadier D F Harris ADC
*Director Equipment Support 5*
Brigadier P A D Evans OBE
*Commander Headquarters Royal Logistic Corps Training Centre*
Brigadier M G R Hodson CBE
*Director of Transport and Movements (Army)*
Brigadier P D Foxton
*Commandant Base Ordnance Depot Donnington*
Brigadier I P Inshaw
*Commandant Base Ordnance Depot Bicester*
Brigadier K J W Goad
*Director Base Depots*
Brigadier T McG Brown OBE
*Director and Chief Executive Defence Postal and Courier Services*
Brigadier A W Pollard
*Director Logistic Information Systems (Army)*
Brigadier R E Ratazzi
*Commander Gutersloh Garrison*
Brigadier P A Chambers MBE
*Director Logistic Support Policy*
Brigadier M Kerley QGM
*Commander Services Support Group (United Kingdom)*

**Medical Discharge Scheme.** Thank you for informing me of my entitlement of £500.00 under the Medical Discharge Grant Scheme. Please find enclosed my bank details. Could you please send the cheque to my bank to be lodged in my account.
*A letter from a serving soldier discharged on medical grounds* February 1995

**Honours and Awards**
The following awards have been made to members of The Royal Logistic Corps since formation:
**New Year's Honours List:**

**Companion of the Order of the Bath**
Major General A L Meier
**Commander of the Order of the British Empire:**
Brigadier A W Lyons
**Officer of the Order of the British Empire:**
Lieutenant Colonel D M Anderson
Lieutenant Colonel P L P Douglas
Lieutenant Colonel G K Geddie
Lieutenant Colonel S F Owen
**Member of the Order of the British Empire:**
Major M I Dolamore
Major J R Donovan
Major M R Lilley
Major (now Lieutenant Colonel) G J Meacher
Captain J W Kendall
Warrant Officer One R M Cainan
Warrant Officer Two (Acting Warrant Officer One) A J Gullis
Warrant Officer Two (Acting Warrant Officer One) L G Jones
Warrant Officer Two (Acting Warrant Officer One) J Seymour
Warrant Officer Two P P Woods
Staff Sergeant (now Warrant Officer Two) T A J Bennett
Staff Sergeant J Eaton (V)
Staff Sergeant (Local Warrant Officer Two) R V C Pearce
Sergeant S J Baldwin
Sergeant M Smith

LEFT: Members of the Mount Kinabalu Expedition, February 1993; RIGHT: hill walking in the Himalayas (The Island at the Top of the World). BELOW: Sub-aqua expedition in Bermuda, led by Major Tim Woodman (157 (Wales and Midlands) Transport Regiment (V)).

**Queen's Birthday Honours:**

**Companion of the Order of the Bath:**
Major General G W Field (Colonel Commandant)

**Commander of the Order of the British Empire:**
Brigadier M A Browne

**Officer of the Order of the British Empire:**
Lieutenant Colonel (Acting Colonel) C R Elderton
Lieutenant Colonel M Kane
Lieutenant Colonel C Robinson BEM
Lieutenant Colonel A Young

**Member of the Order of the British Empire:**
Lieutenant Colonel R M Cannons
Major I W Abbott
Major D J R Martin
Major J P Newis-Edwards
Major R W J Oldham
Captain J A Field
Captain P G Rutherford
Warrant Officer One C N Hedley
Warrant Officer One P J Wise
Warrant Officer Two G A Barker
Warrant Officer Two B J J Cooney (V)
Warrant Officer Two D F Long
Warrant Officer Two J McC Millsip
Warrant Officer Two P R Ogden
Staff Sergeant T M Appleby (V)
Staff Sergeant J Grant
Staff Sergeant W P Theobald (V)
Sergeant S J Bean
Sergeant C Greenwood (V)
Sergeant D Middleton (V)
Corporal M G S Cullen

**For Service in Northern Ireland:**

**Commander of the Order of the British Empire:**
Colonel (now Brigadier) M G R Hodson

**Officer of the Order of the British Empire:**
Lieutenant Colonel (now Colonel) O T Hall
Lieutenant Colonel (Acting Colonel) R Rook
Lieutenant Colonel R A Swindley

**Member of the Order of the British Empire:**
Major A D Farrow
Major I A Jones
Major H E McMahon
Major G A O'Sullivan
Major P R Saddleton
Major S P Smith
Captain P M Swift
Warrant Officer One C D Caffrey
Warrant Officer One D Cottrill
Warrant Officer One W D G Goodchild
Warrant Officer One (Staff Sergeant Major) W D G Hunt
Warrant Officer One R W Travers
Warrant Officer One P M Williams
Corporal M G Newby

**George Medal:**
Warrant Officer (now Acting Captain) J R T Balding

**Queen's Gallantry Medal:**
Major A R Wallace
Captain P G Smith
Warrant Officer One R J McLelland
Warrant Officer Two N MacDonald
Warrant Officer Two (SQMS) R A Wharton
Staff Sergeant (Acting Warrant Officer Two) A N Joy
Lance Corporal W Cuckson

**Queen's Commendation for Bravery:**
Captain A G T J McVey
Warrant Officer Two S Irving
Lance Corporal S W Cocking

**Queen's Commendation for Valuable Service:**
Captain M T Haverty

**Mentioned in Despatches:**
Captain A McArthur
Staff Sergeant D R Dixon
Staff Sergeant A T Fish
Staff Sergeant McCreanor

**GOC's Commendation:**
Captain C Snaith
Sergeant J C Julious

ABOVE: Major N F G Brehaut's team on the summit of Island Peak in the Himalayas, 1993. BELOW: 'C'mon, lads, you can't hold hands for ever!' Adventurous training in the South of France, 1994 (4 General Support Regiment).

127

**For Service in the Former Republic of Yugoslavia :**

**Officer of the Order of the British Empire:**
Lieutenant Colonel D R Ells
Lieutenant Colonel R J Morrison
Lieutenant Colonel J R Wallace MBE
**Member of the Order of the British Empire:**
Captain P A Jones
Warrant Officer Two R A Straney
Staff Sergeant A J Bonney
Staff Sergeant P S Bristo
Sergeant M Macrury

**Queen's Commendation for Valuable Service:**
Major D J R Martin MBE
Captain S J Mackenzie
Corporal P M Impleton
**Mentioned in Despatches:**
Lieutenant Colonel M D Wood MBE
Lance Corporal T Byrne

**Joint Commanders' Commendation (Former Republic of Yugoslavia):**
Major L A Bower
Major S Gray
Major C H Maginnis
Captain P Foley
Sergeant S J Cole
Corporal G R Donalson
Lance Corporal P Wallbridge
**Mention in Despatches:**
Captain R L Maybery QGM
Lieutenant (now Captain) P G Smith
Corporal S Tappin
For Service in Cambodia:
**Member of the Order of the British Empire:**
Captain I A Gordon

## The Corps Grace

For the food and drink we are about to receive
and the skill of those who prepare and serve it,
May the Lord make us truly grateful.
Amen.

ABOVE: The Mayor of Camden taking the salute as the Chelsea Pensioners and 20 Squadron personnel march past during the annual church parade (20 Transport Squadron). BELOW: Corps Coach leaving Guildhall for the Cartmarking Ceremony of the Worshipful Company of Carmen, 1993.

# UNIT IMPRESSIONS & EXPERIENCES

The unit impressions and experiences which follow should be set in the context of change – change of cap badge, change of unit, change of country in the drawdown and closure of overseas units, and finally change of jobs on redundancy. These notes come from a wide variety of units and individuals and they reflect the first years as seen from that level.

**QMG Efficiency Incentive Awards.** In June 1992 the Quartermaster General, General Sir John Learmont KCB CBE, established his efficiency incentive award scheme whereby up to £20,000 a year could be awarded to a range of organisations in his Top Level Budget area for quantifiable efficiency initiatives.

During a recent visit to Base Ammunition Depot Kineton and the Army School of Ammunition, the Quartermaster General presented two awards and certificates. The Directorate of Land Services Ammunition won an award of £10,000 for improvements to methods of reliability data capture and analysis after ammunition proof firings. The second award of £2,500 was presented to Lieutenant Colonel A V Glasby OBE GM, on behalf of Colonel C Field GM, the Commandant Base Ammunition Depot Longtown, where a refurbishment programme of ex-Op Granby unit load containers for ammunition resulted in a saving of £250,000 in disposal and replacement costs.

**Larger Corps – Larger Signs?** In preparation for the creation of The Royal Logistic Corps orders were placed for new unit signs. Somewhere in the order process feet became metres, an increase of three plus. The arrival of the new signs provoked many humorous comments. Below is a record of one such conversation

Sergeant F: Can I ask a question?

Corporal M: You're wondering why the signs are so big. Well, as so many units have changed title it has become a necessity for units to be spotted from the nearest satellite.

Sergeant F: Yes, but ...

Corporal M: Additionally, when dismounted the sign doubles as a helicopter landing pad.

Sergeant F: Yes, but ...

Corporal M: Finally, as we ourselves draw down, the scrap value of our signs will cover the cost of our closing party.

Sergeant F: Yes, but ...

Corporal M: But what?!

Sergeant F: How the heck do we get back inside the building?

*Headquarters Squadron, Theatre Drawdown Unit Germany*

**Ex–Op Granby Ammunition Refurbishment.** After Op Granby 35,000 tonnes of unused ammunition were returned from the Gulf to ammunition depots in the United Kingdom and Germany. A significant proportion of the stock had been removed from its storage containers as ready to use ammunition or transported and stored in the harsh desert environment. The Directorate Land Service Ammunition assessed the condition of all returned stock as suspect and a major ammunition repair and refurbishment programme was initiated in all the Base Ammunition Depots in UK and Germany in September 1991. It was to be completed by 31 March 1994.

It is to the credit of the Corps that the programme was completed slightly ahead of schedule in February 1994. Over 51,500,000 rounds of all ammunition types were returned and over ninety-three per cent was restored to a serviceable condition. By refurbishing the returned ammunition the saving to the Ministry of Defence was in excess of £700 million in replacement costs. This was a major achievement on which the Corps can look with pride.

*Directorate of Land Service Ammunition*

**The Corps goes Independent.** By stealth and manoeuvre Headquarters 20 Armoured Brigade in Paderborn is slowly being infiltrated by The Royal Logistic Corps. With seventy-five per cent of the brigade staff, The Royal Logistic Corps can now lay claim to an Independent Royal Logistic Corps Armoured brigade. G3 snobs need not apply for future positions.

*Headquarters 20 Armoured Brigade*

ABOVE: Lieutenant General Sir Jeremy Mackenzie thanks the members of the HQ ARRC Move to Rheindahlen Team. BELOW: A variety of wheels taking a break in Bosnia (4 General Support Regiment).

**It's Been a Moving Time Since Then.** In April 1993 8 Regiment became 8 Artillery Support Regiment The Royal Logistic Corps. It was to be a year of new beginnings as 12 Squadron embarked on pre–Northern Ireland training.

This was to be the first time a squadron deploying on an Operation Banner roulement tour was to include female soldiers as Saxon and APV drivers in support of infantry troops. 12 Squadron was also to be the last transport squadron to use Moscow Camp as its command headquarters location.

In all 262 officers and soldiers deployed to the Province in October 1993, thirty–one of whom were female. They were employed in driving roles Province–wide, most notably in support of the infantry units in Londonderry and Belfast. The only restriction on employment was that imposed by lack of accommodation. This being a first in a new Corps, many eyes were on the squadron, which completed a very successful tour.

In July 1994 the regiment departed Munster and began the lengthy job of relocating to the recently renamed Marne Barracks in Catterick, North Yorkshire. As the regiment settles in to its new home many look back and ask, 'Where have the last two years gone? And what does the future hold?'

Following the farewell parade in Coerde the regiment hosted a reception in Portsmouth Barracks Officers' Mess, in which the Commanding Officer, Lieutenant Colonel A B Barton, representing the regiment, was presented with an aerial photograph of the town of Coerde by Herr Holland, a great friend of the regiment for many years. Herr Holland was presented with a silver Scorpion statuette from the regiment as a token of appreciation for that friendship.
*8 Artillery Support Regiment*

**Interesting Times.** 'We live in interesting times', according to the currently over–used Chinese proverb. Surely even the most inscrutable of Taoist philosophers would have used a slightly more robust adjective than 'interesting' to describe this regiment's short but frenetic existence. Having rebadged from the Royal Corps of Transport on 5 April, whilst fully occupied with all drawdown movements for 3 and 4 Armoured Divisions, the regiment entered (or disappeared up) its own drawdown tube, as the experts like to call it. The unit is set to amalgamate with its sister regiment to become 24 Regiment on 1 June. There, sounds easy doesn't it? That simple sentence makes no reference to evicting the Station Staff Officer from Block 2, taking a sledgehammer to several office walls, rewiring the telephone system, drawing down two Armoured Divisions, one Mobile Civilian Transport Group unit and one Mixed Service Organisation unit, opening a new airport, receiving rifle 5.56mm into service, changing all stationery and over a dozen unit signs twice in eight weeks and maintaining routine tasking, all without 'taking your eye off the Balkans'.Reflect awhile on the fact that we will be the first unit in the Corps to disband, as well as being one of, if not the, shortest lived regiments in the British Army, in peacetime. Sort of makes it all worth while really, doesn't it? Right, where's that paintbrush?
*25 Transport and Movements Regiment*

**Loco Naming.** On Wednesday 26 May 1993 Royal Mail in conjunction with British Rail honoured The Royal Logistic Corps by naming British Rail main line diesel locomotive 47568, *Royal Logistic Corps Postal and Courier Services* in recognition of the formation of the new Corps.

A special train named *The Logistician*, consisting of nine Mk 2 air-conditioned 1st class open saloons coaches and a Travelling Post Office, complete with crew and 'live' mail, was chartered for the day.
*Postal & Courier Services*

**Feeding the Hungry Multitude.** Background: 'Would it not be a good idea for Dhekelia Garrison to host a Panayiri (Greek for village party) and invite all of our civilian workers as

LEFT: Private Tarne 'happy as a sandboy' (7 Transport Regiment);
RIGHT: Half frozen (Catering Group). BELOW: Captains Yates and Rose
playing battleships on exercise (7 Transport Regiment).

well as villagers from the local area?' The Garrison Quartermaster's first question was to ask whether there was a precedent for feeding 5,000 people in one sitting – apparently there was, but it was a long time ago and involved some chap with three loaves of bread and five fishes.

After the Panayiri the following was overheard in the Officers' Mess: 'The Dhekelia Panayiri was such a great success, that I shall recommend to my sucessor that it be held every two years'. Any Warrant Officer (Catering) who hopes to serve as the Area Catering Warrant Officer Dhekelia in the future would be well advised to keep this article (in the *Corps Journal* of October 1993) as an aide memoire.

*Warrant Officer One A G Bradshaw MBE, Cyprus.*

**Manpower High and Low.** 23 Pioneer Regiment is a unique regiment within the Corps. Unlike most units, we have neither a large fleet of trucks nor an impressive stores inventory. Instead we provide, across all three Services, that most precious commodity, manpower. The regiment consists of HQ Squadron and two field force squadrons at Bicester and a third field force squadron located, at present, at Kineton.

At any given time, we have men deployed around the globe providing Pioneer Support wherever and whenever required. At present (1993) we have troops in Bosnia and Croatia, Belize, Canada, the Falkland Islands, Northern Ireland, Australia and New Zealand. We have recently had a troop return from Gibraltar and in August a squadron goes to Cyprus and a troop to Denmark.

*23 Pioneer Regiment*

**A Job Well Done. A Fuel Tanker Driver Earns his Pay in Bosnia.** Once up and about the fuel driver is ready for anything, mostly a good breakfast followed by a cup of tea. The convoy quickly prepares itself to leave, the convoy commander makes his final checks, making sure the drivers are lined up ready to leave the Dalma vehicle park in Split. They prepare for a barrage of questions: 'Got your rifle? Got your mags? Got your helmet? Got your flak jacket? Got your rations? Got your bergen? Got your brain?' The response is usually swift, although some are hesitant on the last one.

So the convoy moves off. The convoy commander gets straight on the radio and starts abusing the sensitivity of his eardrums. The Land Rover driver starts flapping his arms outside his window and shouting 'Ja sam lude' to oncoming traffic. He has been told by his convoy commander that this means 'Slow down', when it really means 'I am crazy', but the effect on the locals is the same: a crazy British squaddie waving his arms out of a Land Rover in a bizarre attempt to take off, shouting, 'I am crazy', quickly followed by about ten noisy fuel tankers and a cloud of black exhaust fumes. It normally gets them to slow down though.

The routes into Bosnia are varied, but whichever way we go the drivers soon find themselves on hilly, twisty, bendy roads. After a few hours on the road the convoy commander uses his elite map-reading skills and finds a suitable place to pull over for the first vehicle check. Our first stop is in Gornji Vakuf and, if we have not had many breakdowns we normally push straight up to Vitez. If we make it out of Gornji Vakuf alive we start what is normally the last two hours of the journey to Vitez. This takes us up Route Diamond, which starts off by cutting its way through a ghost town of burnt out-houses.

The mudbath they call a bulk fuel installation at Vitez is a welcome sight for tired drivers, but not the end of their day. Unloading fuel can take many hours and, while the convoy commander sorts out the paperwork, his 2IC takes over and coordinates the unloading and parking. All this is done by torchlight and I am not the first to step into a four foot deep mud hole. The night is spent either on a gym floor or in a small transit room. If you are extremely lucky you might get a lukewarm shower at Vitez.

The next morning starts off with a fight for the wash basins and a cold water shave, a quick trip in a 4-tonner to Bulk Fuel

ABOVE: Corps 1994 Methuen Cup team, with Major General D L Burden
CBE and Major D J Owen. BELOW: Army Golf Champions 1994. Lance
Corporal Stevenson, Private Ashby, Warrant Officer Two Gray and
Warrant Officer One Oliver (Captain).

Installation 2 and preparation for the move back to Split. The convoy commander dishes out his orders and again goes through his checklist, which now includes, 'Got your cork?'. The last chance to go to the toilet is at Gornji Vakuf.

We can usually get some enjoyment at the MALBAT bridge. The Malaysians who control the bridge, which was destroyed in the fighting and rebuilt by Engineers, always stop us and ask the same questions: 'Where you go?' 'How many vehicles?' and 'Where you from?' Confuse them with answering the last one by saying, 'Warrington, mate', and he normally comes back with 'Warblington?' and I say, 'Hi' very sharply and drive off saying, 'Very roomy, very economical'. Its good for morale.

The arrival in Split is normally at night and the job is not finished until everything is parked up and put away. If we have got back with no breakdowns and no accidents it's a bonus, but at the end of the day it's a job well done.

*Corporal Stu Vernon, Brit Transport Squadron, BRITLOGBAT in Bosnia*

## The First Year of the Specialist.

On 5 April 1993 the RLC TA in Grantham came into existence. By this time a lot of preparation work had taken place. During the build-up officers and soldiers of the Forming Corps had been posted in to what was then HQ RCT TA at Prince William of Gloucester Barracks to prepare the way for their units.

For many members of the Forming Corps change was going to be difficult. Old haunts were being left, old friends lost and new ones had to be made, however at Grantham there was a warm welcome for all. The facilities are excellent for training. Initially there was little cross-posting between the different functions, but as the year progressed the barriers were eroded. The Specialist RLC TA will gain 1,000 posts and reorganisation will involve the raising of a Transport Group Headquarters,

two Transport Regiments, a Port Regiment, a Movement Control Regiment, together with the formation of a Support Regiment and a Pioneer Regiment from the regrouping of current assets.

Grantham has rapidly become the 'Drill Hall' for the largest Specialist TA element in the Army. The infrastructure is being extended to cope with the additional numbers, and to move is to trip over a workman or two.

*Lieutenant Colonel M R U McCartney, Headquarters RLC Territorial Army, Grantham*

## Going Forward Together In The South Atlantic.

I was heavily involved in the formation of The Royal Logistic Corps in Hong Kong where, with a lot of goodwill, everything went very smoothly. PB10 obviously saw my potential as a Royal Logistic Corps crusader and so they dispatched me to the Falkland Islands in January 1994. My job as the SO2 J4 Logistics (Operations and Plans) has given me the opportunity to see, and in some cases experience, almost every functional area that our Corps has to offer at first hand. I have seen Corps Chefs in South Georgia who produced superb meals despite working in a kitchen which would not look out of place in a 'Flintstones' film. With Royal Logistic Corps 'Posties', I have helped sort the mail, which arrives twice a week (if we're lucky) in the Tristar from UK. I've been on a tour round Mare Harbour in a Landing Craft Vehicle Personnel courtesy of 460 Port Troop. The Ordnance Squadron provides the theatre with its rations and ammunition and in addition has a 'stitch' who repairs anything from Goretex trousers to arctic smocks. The RAF POL Flight has a Royal Logistic Corps Petroleum Operator, who virtually runs the Petroleum Depot. There are also Air Movers, Butchers, Ammunition Technicians, Vehicle Specialists, Supply Controllers, Supply Specialists as well as Drivers from Aldershot-based 27 Transport Regiment.

ABOVE: The Regimental Pipes and Drums of 152 (Ulster) Ambulance
Regiment (V), 1994. BELOW: 151 (Greater London) Support Regiment
(V) provides a UN display during the 1994 Lord Mayor's Show.

The Falkland Islands theatre relies heavily on the professionalism of the soldiers of The Royal Logistic Corps. Without their skills and excellent attitude this theatre could not function. We have now ensured that the few remaining signs and badges of the five Forming Corps have gone from public view, and we are going forward together here. This is a theatre where The Royal Logistic Corps has a major role to play and it is true that here 'We Sustain'. We have a real job to do and in the South Atlantic we are doing it really well.
*Major A D Stevens, Headquarters Falkland Islands*

**Northern Ireland: A Changing Province.**
The months which have elapsed since the birth of The Royal Logistic Corps have seen great changes and developments within the regiment. The regiment is a widely dispersed unit, with RHQ and 26 Transport Squadron located in Lisburn, 84 Postal & Courier Squadron located at Aldergrove and 57 Supply Squadron and the Roulement Transport Squadron located at Kinnegar. 21 Regiment encompasses the whole spectrum of RLC operations.

For many the greatest change in Northern Ireland has been the departure after twenty-one years of the Roulement Transport Squadron from Moscow Camp in April 1994. The squadron headquarters has relocated to Kinnegar Logistic Base and its size reduced on the formation of E Troop 26 Transport Squadron, which took over the GT Troop functions of the Roulement Squadron.

Many members of the Corps will have happy memories of serving in 'Slipper City', even if their time there was spent on the Regimental Police shift following a road traffic accident. A debt of gratitude is due to Major David Owen, the last Camp Commandant, who kept the camp ticking over.

**Operations.** The regiment's 'normal' logistic operations include holding an average of 1300 vehicles, valued at £7 million, providing transport Province-wide and handling just under 35,000 inbound and 17,000 outbound mailbags a year.

In addition the regiment has also carried out a number of larger scale short term operations, including the provision of transport for engineer stores and plant in support of the rebuild of Crossmaglen and Newtownhamilton Security Bases. Both of these operations have involved large convoys deep into the heart of bandit country.

The regiment has also successfully backloaded and inloaded numerous vehicles using the LSLs *Sir Tristram* and *Sir Percival*. The fact that these operations went without a hitch was due in part to Regimental Ops/149 Movement Control Troop actually being at work – all at once.

**Conclusion.** With peace breaking out in the Province the future is not yet clear; however, within our first two years as a regiment in the new Corps we have achieved a great deal.
*21 Logistic Support Regiment*

**Branded by the Lord Mayor of London.**
Nobody really knew what to expect when the Royal Corps of Transport, Royal Army Ordnance Corps, Royal Pioneer Corps and Army Catering Corps were amalgamated. The idea of a Chef driving a tank transporter and a Trucker making a beef stroganoff was not one to be cherished, however the amalgamation took place on 5 April 1993 and life went on.

As a member of 25 Freight Distribution Squadron, life has not changed much at all. New drivers, mainly ex-Royal Army Ordnance Corps, turned up and drove the vehicles in a professional manner.

The Worshipful Company of Carmen is an organisation that dates back to the twelfth century and mainly involves itself with transportation matters. The Master is elected annually by the governing, elected court. 25 Squadron is honoured to be the 'Carmen's Own.' The Cart Marking Ceremony is an echo of past times, registering vehicles plying for hire, a bit like collecting your car tax from the Post Office, except that this ceremony takes place in the Guildhall Courtyard in London and a wooden plaque on the side of the

ABOVE: 'Well, the troop commander told me to follow him' (14 Transport Squadron). LEFT: Supply Detachment in Vitez (4 General Support Regiment). RIGHT: Cam cream faces, wet feet (9 Supply Regiment).

139

vehicle is branded with the year date by the Lord Mayor of London. There was a great procession of vehicles and I was proud to represent 25 Squadron with our vehicle.

This year has been a busy and enjoyable one for me. I am sure, with time, we will all do as well together in The Royal Logistic Corps as we all did in our previous Corps. So here's to The Royal Logistic Corps.

*Lance Corporal Campbell, 25 Freight Distribution Squadron (The Carmen's)*

**Frustrating the Bomber.** In 1969, in response to an increasing terrorist bombing campaign, the Army began to reinforce its bomb disposal unit in Northern Ireland. Over twenty-five years later, and now known as 321 Explosive Ordnance Disposal Squadron, The Royal Logistic Corps, the unit remains the only agency permitted to investigate and render safe suspect improvised explosive devices in the Province. The squadron is manned by officers and soldiers of the Regular Army, predominantly Ammunition Technicians from The Royal Logistic Corps, supported by personnel from other trades within the Corps, the Royal Signals, the Infantry and the Adjutant General's Corps.

Prior to the formation of The Royal Logistic Corps in April 1993 our predecessors in the Royal Army Ordnance Corps dealt with over 43,965 emergency calls, about forty calls a week. Of these calls over 5,183 were real devices and led to the recovery of 256,026 kg of explosives. Since the formation of The Royal Logistic Corps the squadron has attended 2,347 emergency calls, about thirty-two calls a week, and recovered 12,517 kg of explosive prior to the Provisional Irish Republican Army ceasefire on 31 August 1994.

The Provisional Irish Republican Army Mark 16 mortar was the newest arrival in the nationalist terrorist armoury, being first deployed on 13 July 1993 in Londonderry. It has been deployed thirty-three times throughout the Province and consists of a mortar bomb containing 900 grammes of Semtex, a launch tube, a length of firing cable and a firing pack.

The Protestant paramilitaries increased their use of the bomb during the spring of 1994 and deployed a comprehensive range of Improvised Explosive Devices.

The squadron has lost twenty of its members killed on operations in the Province. Since formation one operator has been injured. A reflection of the coverage and dedication of Explosive Ordnance Disposal operators and other squadron members is the high number of gallantry awards held by the squadron. 321 Explosive Ordnance Disposal Squadron RLC is the most decorated peace time unit in the British services, with 299 awards for gallantry including two George Crosses, twenty-nine George Medals and sixty-one Queen's Gallantry Medals. Ammunition Technical Officers now come from a far wider background and the squadron will no doubt benefit from its more cosmopolitan composition.

*321 Explosive Ordnance Disposal Squadron*

**Two-wheeled Cross-Overs.** Started in 1969 The Blue Arrows Motor Cycle Display Team is well-known in communities both large and small across Scotland and has performed a number of times in the South of England. Local galas and major events such as The Royal Highland Show have hosted the team and have had crowds shouting for more. Between May and September last year The Blue Arrows turned out to over thirty locations, sometimes performing two or three times daily.

Its 25th anniversary year in 1994 saw the arrival of new motor cycles, eight Kawasaki KLX 250cc, which replaced eight of the older KLR models. Our twelve man team, recruited from soldiers throughout the regiment, thrill the public with their skilful ground formation riding and specialist routines, such as their famous zipper, and car and fire jumps, as well as the odd 'wheelie' thrown in for good measure. If you have not seen them you have missed something.

*The Blue Arrows Motor Cycle Display Team. The Scottish Transport Regiment (V)*

ABOVE: Major P Towndrow, Lieutenants G Moverley, P Martin, and
T Burgess on a mountaineering expedition in southern Russia, 1994.
BELOW: 1993 Army fencing champions (3 Base Ammunition Depot).

**The Children from Chernobyl.** In early September 1994, the Paderborn Catering Office received a strange request for catering support at a camp for forty-nine deaf and dumb children from the Chernobyl area of Russia. The camp is an annual event hosted by the German community in the Harz Mountains near Bad Lauterberg.

It was soon evident that there were no experts on Soviet cuisine, let alone any Russian speakers, within the Paderborn area. So, with some head scratching, two chefs were identified and despatched with pans and cooksets to the campsite, Lance Corporal Burnside from 2nd Battalion Light Infantry and, to complete the international flavour, Sergeant Jarvis, who is a member of the Australian Army here in Germany on an exchange visit.

After the initial settling in period, the children warmed to the staff and it was not long before nicknames were allotted to those children with unpronounceable names.

Any initial worries about menu suitability were soon dispelled as the children enthusiastically tucked into whatever was put in front of them, with their favourite dishes being burgers and roast dinners with all the trimmings. There was also some cross-fertilization of ideas as one of the Russian aides demonstrated some of their local Russian dishes such as pancakes with cream cheese and mince; however it was the content and quality of the English cuisine that won the day and the children were soon eating fried breakfasts and more of our traditional dishes as the camp entered its third week.

Although communication was difficult a bond soon grew between the staff and children and the chefs were always invited to accompany them on the many organised excursions. As a result of the many friendships that developed there was quite an emotional farewell barbeque prior to the children departing, clutching their packed meals for a three day journey back to their homes in Russia.

*Logistic Support Branch (Catering), Headquarters 20 Armoured Brigade*

**New Name. Old Job. And a Move to Boot.** For a long time Defence Company Royal Pioneer Corps had been an integral part of the 1 (BR) Corps set up in Bielefeld. Following the demise of 1 (BR) Corps and the subsequent formation of the Allied Command Europe Rapid Reaction Corps (ARRC) and its Support Battalion the continuing role of the Defence Company was assured. The formation of The Royal Logistic Corps on 5 April 1993 gave rise to the Defence Company being re-titled 170 Pioneer Squadron RLC.

170 Pioneer Squadron forms part of HQ ARRC's Support Battalion alongside 14 Transport Squadron and Headquarters Company, who together provide logistic support to HQ ARRC. The squadron consists of five officers, five senior ranks and ninety-five junior ranks, who are structured into Squadron Headquarters and three troops. Its role is to provide security and labour support to the headquarters, both in peace and on operations.

In terms of commitments the squadron is always busy providing security to JHQ, labour support to HQ ARRC plus all manner of support to various outside agencies.

*170 Pioneer Squadron*

**The Key to the World (or the Three Ugly Sisters).** 29 Regiment deployed on five operations in the first year, including Op Warden, Op Hamden and Grapple, as well as in support of countless United Kingdom Land Forces exercises worldwide. It was a shock to all at first that the hardest working squadron in the regiment transpired to be 80 Postal & Courier Squadron, the remnants of the now disbanded 2 Postal & Courier Regiment Royal Engineers.

ABOVE: DROPS vehicles above Ramsko Jezero Lake, Staff Sergeant Graham Jack being interviewed (27 Tranpsort Regiment). (Courtesy of The Scottish Daily Record and Sunday Mail Ltd) BELOW: Corporal Gowans (8 Squadron) leads another convoy back south on Route Triangle in Bosnia (27 Transport Regiment). (Courtesy of *Soldier* Magazine)

143

At the first regimental dinner night after the loyal toast and walnuts (walnuts?!) had been served it soon became apparent that a heated discussion was taking place between three of the Officer Commandings, Officer Commanding 47 Air Despatch Squadron, Officer Commanding 55 Movement Control Squadron and Officer Commanding 80 Postal & Courier Squadron. The Officer Commanding 47 Squadron was insisting in his Irish brogue that the postal trade was without a doubt the Cinderella of the trades within the regiment. Officer Commanding 80 Squadron immediately agreed, gleefully pointing out that Cinderella had two large, spoilt and ugly sisters.

This dinner was also unique in being a mixed Officers' and Sergeants' Mess affair. So successful was it that the dinner will be repeated each April in commemoration of the formation. It was also the first occasion when the Winged Key was present on the table decoration. This logistic key, with the number XXIX as the teeth of the key and a wing to the centre, indicates our world wide and air support role. We truly are 'The Key to the World' for United Kingdom Land Army.
*Captain S D Glynn, 29 Regiment*

**What's in a Name?** Unlike so many of our sister organisations that operate within the depot framework, the change of Corps from Royal Army Ordnance Corps to The Royal Logistic Corps was made on the 5 April 1993 with the loss of a numerical unit prefix and regimental title. The Army Establishments Committee had recommended that the new unit title should be Base Ordnance Depot Donnington Support Unit, which became BDSU for short, and so, like the ugly duckling we hid in the bullrushes (metaphorically speaking of course) until something better could be agreed.

During the intervening period, many changes and achievements were made by the men and women serving in this unit, the most notable of which was that we were to become the first minor unit ever to win a Combined Services tug-of-war championships title (under 600 kilogrammes). This achievement is even more remarkable when the strength of the unit is considered. As 15 Battalion RAOC the unit strength was 320, however, on reorganisation to BDSU our strength was reduced to 247 and, if undermanning and other factors were considered, an effective total of 180 was nearer the truth. This reduction has had the knock-on effect of giving the majority of personnel more than one job, an unusual state of affairs in the modern army.
*15 Regiment*

**Cookery Training Department.** Since the formation of the Corps the Cookery Training Department of the Army School of Catering has retained its primary role, teaching all technical aspects of catering for the army. These areas are covered in a number of courses:

RLC Chef Class 2: Apprentice Training
Adult recruit (to include Royal Irish)
Butchery Duties Course: All Arms Course
Territorial Army B3-B1: Territorial Army personnel Royal Logistic Corps Chef Class 1: Corps NCOs Chef to Senior Officer's Residence

We have recently seen some outstanding successes:

July 1993: The Army Team competed in Hungary, a Military Culinary Competition in both cold buffet work and field cookery aspects. January-February 1994: World of Hospitality. Junior Salon: Best Junior Entry in Show (twenty-two medals). Senior Salon: Gold Medal winners. Parade of Chefs: Army School of Catering. Identiboard Trophy: Most Hygienic Kitchen. Services Chef of the Year: Sergeant P Weaver. National Chef of the Year: Warrant Officer Class 1 (SSM) L Jones MBE.

ABOVE: A successful running squad from 82 Airborne General Support Squadron, 1994. BELOW: Corps tug-of-war champions (560 kg and 640 kg) in 1993 (17 Port & Maritime Regiment).

The Army Team, led by Warrant Officer Class 1 Jones MBE, competed in the Military Culinary World Cup in Luxembourg in November 1994. The team were all Royal Logistic Corps Chef Instructors at the Army School of Catering. They not only had to cook the meal but market it as well. They had to persuade visitors to buy tickets for their meal and the number of tickets sold contributed towards their overall marks. They did this by cooking a sample of the menu in advance and displaying it in a glass cabinet outside the kitchen from the beginning of the preparation period. Their success just goes to prove that most people eat with their eyes.

Cold Buffet: Silver Medal; Hot Menu: Gold Medal; Overall Position: Runner-Up

The overall winners of the Military World Cup by a small margin were the Dutch team.
*Army School of Catering*

**The Skirl of the Pipes.** The Pipes and Drums of the Scottish Transport Regiment formed on 5 April 1993 with the amalgamation of 153 (Highland) and 154 (Lowland) Regiments RCT(V). All Band members were in fact members of 153 Regiment, whose Pipes and Drums trace their history back to 1937, further than any other band in the Corps except the Regular Staff Band.

They have played at most of the Corps functions and last year competed for the first time since 1984 in the Territorial Army Pipe Band Competition. In these first two years the Band has doubled in size.

The Band also played in Fort Eustis in Virginia, USA, at both military and civilian functions, including General Whalley's annual garden party. They were also resident pipe band for the Williamsburg Scottish Festival where, against strong competition, they achieved two firsts, two seconds and a third in the Open Solo Piping Competition. The Band is continuing to expand and demands for performances are overwhelming.
*The Scottish Transport Regiment (V)*

**The Channel Tunnel.** Since the formation of The Royal Logistic Corps two years ago, modern technology has presented the Explosive Ordnance Disposal world with many challenging tasks, none more so than those encountered at the Channel Tunnel. Whilst the eyes of the world marvelled at an engineering masterpiece, soldiers from The Royal Logistic Corps strove to protect it and plan for the future.

Of course, the idea of a fixed link between Britain and the European mainland dates back to Napoleonic times. Since then plan after plan has been suggested and in 1880 the beginnings of the inaugural tunnel were formed, only to be aborted two years later after British fears of invasion became too great.

It soon became necessary to call upon the skills of Ammunition Technicians. Their initial task was to render safe the hundreds of conventional munitions discovered by the 'Tunnel Tigers' as they dug up an area of the Kent countryside renowned for being home to various British and Canadian ranges.

In the meantime, contingency planning was well under way to counter any threat posed by terrorists, cranks or criminals to disrupt either the building or efficient running of the Tunnel. Already it was obvious that the Channel Tunnel would present challenges never before encountered by 11 Explosive Ordnance Disposal Regiment. Although the EOD role was to remain the protection of life, the safeguarding of property and the preservation of forensic evidence (in that order of priority), problems such as team deployment, a hostile environment and portability were all to prove particularly demanding.

The Running Tunnels form 105 kilometres of track, travelling over 100 metres below sea level in depth. This makes for a cold, dark environment with minimal movement space, which is further confounded by a lethal 25,000 volt power supply running the length of the tunnel. Communication systems would have to be established. Relative blast overpressure calculations proved how particularly hostile

ABOVE: HQ 20 Armoured Brigade RLC. BELOW: 65 Ordnance
Company bakers, with Major David Cousins front right.

this environment could be to an EOD operator.

Overcoming the problems associated with the tunnel itself was only half of the battle, however; the mechanical systems used to travel through the tunnel would have to be examined as well. Three main vehicles would transport traffic across the fixed link: the Eurostar Passenger Train, Le Shuttle Tourist Train and the Heavy Goods Vehicle Carrier Wagon. Trials had to be conducted on each vehicle within International Train Stations, International Terminals and, of course, underground.

In July of 1994, after seven years of work from various Explosive Ordnance Disposal departments and in conjunction with Kent County Constabulary and the Department of Transport's Security Division, these painstaking efforts were put to the test before Eurotunnel 'went public'. The exercise proved extremely successful and showed how 11 Explosive Ordnance Disposal Regiment had once again seen, adapted and overcome major challenges to continue to provide a professional service to its country.

**11 EOD Regiment**

**The 1994 Winter Inload at the British Army Training Unit Suffield.** Every winter, once the exercise season has ended and the battle groups have left, BATUS receives a huge inload of equipment and stores. 1994's inload was considered to be the largest in BATUS history. We received three boats, one for 1995 exercise ammunition, the others bringing accommodation and Engineer stores, operational rations packs, vehicles of all types and general freight.

Prior to the boats arriving we had to prepare and load onto rail flats sixty-five assorted A vehicles which were to be returned to the United Kingdom for base overhaul. This had to be completed in less than a week. It went without a hitch but involved all available manpower from Vehicle and Transport and Movement Troops. Once this was completed Vehicle and Transport and Movement Troop

personnel headed east. 1,300 pallets of ammunition were the first to arrive. Three members of Ammunition Troop travelled to Quebec to help supervise the unloading and then loading the train under the guidance of the Transport and Movement Troop.

The St John boat contained the stores and the A vehicles. It was unloaded on time. The train cars were sent on their way after the accommodation stores, destined for Camp Crowfoot, had been transferred from sea containers to rail box cars.

The third boat arrived a week later and was a routine liner service ship. Vehicle Troop and much of Transport and Movements Troop travelled to Halifax to receive this boat and transfer equipment to rail flats. Having arrived at Halifax, and transferred some vehicles to other users in Canada and the United States, it was decided to drive the BATUS-bound B vehicles to St John to load there. This was completed with the assistance of fifty drivers from the Canadian Forces Base, Gagetown. After a nine hour drive the port was reached safely and work started on the rail loading.

The train to Suffield was three kilometres long and received attention from local TV and newspapers. It moved 129 A vehicles, 82 B and C vehicles and box car after box car of stores. Unfortunately the railhead at Suffield, six miles from BATUS, was not large enough to take the whole train in one go, so first to arrive were the ammunition and Challenger tanks, next came the remaining A vehicles and some general freight. Last but not least came the B vehicles. All were unloaded before Christmas.

Of the 129 A vehicles, 50 or so of the CVR(T)s are destined for the new Opposition Force being introduced for the 1995 season. Arrivals of particular note were the AS90 guns to replace M109 and DROPS to support the battle groups out on the prairie. The inload went well, despite some very cold weather, the vagaries of Canadian Pacific Railway and the usual problems with vehicles suffering from extreme cold.

*Second Lieutenant E Lock, British Army Training Unit Suffield*

ABOVE: A break from the rigorous training programme in Gibraltar, 1994 (156 (North West) Transport Regiment (V)). BELOW: Two wheel and four wheel champions line up (157 (Wales & Midlands) Transport Regiment (V)). (Courtesy of Stephen O'Neill Photography, Cardiff)

**Top Level Budget Move.** On 5 August 1993, just four months after the formation of The Royal Logistic Corps, the Executive Committee of the Army Board directed that four Royal Logistic Corps installations in Germany be transferred from the Top Level Budget of Commander-in-Chief British Army of the Rhine to the Top Level Budget of the Quartermaster General. The units concerned were 3 Base Ammunition Depot, Bracht; 12 Supply Regiment, Wulfen; 14 Supply Regiment, Dulmen and 122 Petroleum Squadron, Warendorf.

From the time that it was decided to transfer the units a further decision was made to close the Petroleum Depot at Warendorf and to relocate 122 Petroleum Squadron. Warendorf was therefore not transferred to the Quartmaster General's Top Level Budget and remained with HQ United Kingdom Support Command (Germany), for closure action to be effected by them.

The units transferred to the control of the Director of Base Depots in Andover on 1 April 1994. To provide him with an appropriate management structure in Germany the Director of Base Depots established a small forward office at Joint Headquarters Rheindahlen, known as DBD (Forward). This office has functional and budgetary control over the units at Bracht, Wulfen and Dulmen, whilst command lies directly with the Director of Base Depots in Andover. The budget for the Director of Base Depots (Forward) units represented some twenty-five per cent of the overall Director of Base Depots budget for 1994. The three units employ some 1,200 civilian and 500 military personnel. 12 and 14 Supply Regiments are Field Army units employed in the base area. The regiments are Army assets whose respective roles are to provide Port of Entry Combat Supplies and Materiel support to a Theatre of Operations.

Defence Costs Study Number 10 recommended the closure of 3 Base Ammunition Depot at Bracht, which will be emptied by 1 April 1996.

*Director of Base Depots (Forward)*

**Inshore Lifeboats at Looe.** On 5 April 1993 154 Ammunition Depot, 4 Petroleum Depot Royal Army Ordnance Corps and four Territorial Army squadrons based in the United Kingdom became 12 Supply Regiment. The new regiment is composed of a Regimental Headquarters, Headquarters Squadron and an Ammunition Squadron based at Wulfen to the north of Essen, a Petroleum Squadron based at Warendorf and four Territorial Army squadrons, two Petroleum Squadrons and an Ammunition Squadron in England and a Rations Squadron in Scotland.

The single most satisfying event in the first twelve months of the regiment was the success of Exercise Mega Triathlon. The aim was to raise enough money to purchase five inshore lifeboats for the Royal National Lifeboat Institution, each to be named after one of the Forming Corps, with the last one to be called *Spirit of The RLC* to mark the *esprit de corps* already present in the new organization. On Saturday 20 August 1994 the Commanding Officer, Lieutenant Colonel Mike Southworth, handed over a cheque to the value of £ 33,000 to the Lifeboat Station at Looe, while his wife, Terry, launched the first of the boats to be commissioned, namely the *Spirit of the RAOC*. The Regimental Colonel and his wife, Christine, and four buglers from 150 Transport Regiment RLC(V) were in attendance. It was indeed a supreme effort by all members of the triathlon team and regimental members who collected all over British Forces Germany to raise funds.

*12 Supply Regiment*

**Our Lambeg Drum.** To commemorate the disbandment of the Royal Corps of Transport two of us decided that we would present the regiment with a special gift. Hours of long, heated conversations took place in the Officers' Mess bar as to what the presentation should be. Major Gerry Shaw and Captain Bill Terret, two self confessed local experts, decided that they would trawl the Province for a large authentic drum.

ABOVE: In the Siwalik Mountains of India (17 Artillery Support Squadron, Exercise Saharanpur Diamond). BELOW: Base Ordnance Depot Donnington, winners of the 1993 Williamson Trophy.

After weeks of searching, we discovered an antique shop in Carrickfergus displaying an original Lambeg Drum, as used on the 12 July Marches during the last few centuries.

We 'coughed up' £250 for this Lambeg Drum and it was restored to its former glory. Renovation and paintwork cost a further £50. Two excited officers organised a formal presentation, dignitaries and all, for the same day as The Drum's scheduled collection.

Imagine the Commanding Officer's surprise when it was explained to the assembled masses that the grand ceremonial presentation had to be cancelled. He was led outside and duly witnessed the most sparklingly restored Salvation Army drum, a £300 embarrassing lesson for the 'local experts'

*152 (Ulster) Ambulance Regiment (V)*

**Still Time to Do It.** Since the amalgamation of the two BAOR Transport and Movement Regiments on 1 June, life within the newly formed 24 Regiment has continued apace. The regiment's commitment to drawdown and the routine operations at Hannover and Munster-Osnabruck airports has remained frenetic. Unbelievably, however, we have participated in a number of other activities, not least two *Fahnenband* parades, the first in Hannover to mark the departure of 24 Transport and Movements Regiment RLC from Hannover.

*24 Regiment*

**Army Caterers Speed Up Theory Testing.** A revolutionary development of database technology which speeds up the process of generating, marking and analysing examination papers has been installed in the Army School of Catering. The system also provides improved student feedback and archives the details of tests and results. The software maintains student details which will follow the individual throughout his or her career. Perhaps the 'Jewel in the Crown', however, is its ability to select questions and compile test papers on a random basis. Set out below are the details of this new and exciting development.

**Question Banks:** Protecting the integrity of question papers has always been a thorny problem. It leads to suspicion about the validity of questions and mistrust that a degree of teaching to tests may occur.

A comprehensive bank of questions has been entered into the database. Each question is coded according to its Training Objective, its Week of Training and the course to which it refers.

**Generation of Examination Papers:** Papers are generated by asking the software to produce a test comprising a given number of questions, from a particular course and reflecting only those training objectives that need to be tested.

**Marking the Papers and Providing Feedback:** There is no longer any need to create answer disks for a particular examination. Once an examination has been generated it will be uniquely identified by subject code, date and squad number. The existing student answer sheets are fed directly into the system. A detailed feedback sheet is delivered for each successful student, showing all those questions that he/she answered incorrectly.

**Improved Analysis:** In order constantly to improve the quality of the question bank an analysis based upon student response to any given question is possible by test and on an historical basis. The system can be interrogated in order to query student results during any appeals or disputes that may arise.

In short we have a testing system which fulfills all of our currently known requirements in this field of theory testing. It saves time which we can put into more thorough assessments and it provides the School with the assurance that our written tests are valid, relevant and up to date.

*Major D Dau, Army School of Catering*

**Same Job - New Title.** The Regional Depot Thatcham continues to provide strong operational and training support to the Field Army at home and overseas on a seamless basis following the formation of the new Corps. All ranks in the Hermitage and

ABOVE: Ammunition Troop, 94 Squadron bombing up 1 PWO at the Cable Factory, Tomislavgrad (National Support Element — Op Grapple). BELOW: Lance Corporal Lamb, thinking he is unobserved, checking the oil in a Land Rover (14 Transport Squadron).

Thatcham station who came together as The Royal Logistic Corps were joined in their celebrations at an outstanding regimental breakfast provided by our Territorial Army colleagues for a number of local dignitaries. The Mayor of Newbury, Counsellor Robert Judge, having unveiled the new depot entrance sign, commented that, although the name had changed work was going on as usual. This led to the report in the local press being headlined, 'Same Job - New Title'.

For other units the change was more marked and the depot was immediately deeply involved in two major events: the Quartermaster General's Launch of The Royal Logistic Corps at Andover, for which the depot provided a considerable breadth of support ranging from a jungle/desert/arctic/ European scenario for the Director of Clothing and Textiles, the Logistic Support Stores for the Premier launch event and a hundred and one things required to make the day a success.
*Regional Depot Thatcham*

**North-West Travel Agents.** Fancy a trip abroad at extremely competitive prices? Then come to 156 (North-West) Transport Regiment (V). In 1994 'holidays' (training) were available in Norway (Exercise Hardfall), France (Exercise Dragons Flight), Belize (Drawdown), Germany (Exercise Pack Saddle and Flying Falcon), Chile (Op Raleigh), Alaska (Op Raleigh) and Gibraltar (Exercise Marble Tor). Just ask members of the regiment for details. As you can see there really is an international flavour about our way of doing business, with trips available to all four corners of the world. We are hoping to expand our scope of operations in 1995. So book early to avoid disappointment..
*156 (North-West) Transport Regiment (V), Liverpool*

**New Corps. New Forest.** The bustling life of 17 Port & Maritime Regiment was punctuated in 1993 by two parades, different in character and mood but both significant milestones in our recent history.

In April 1993 we said farewell to the Royal Corps of Transport, Royal Army Ordnance Corps and Army Catering Corps, not one of the regiment's happiest moments. Changing cap badges and loyalties is a difficult business and, for some in our midst, this was the second time they had been through the process.

The Royal Hampshire Regiment had for a long time been affiliated to the New Forest District – regrettably theirs was another flag to come down in 1993. The Council asked 17 Regiment if we would take their affiliation and, with great pride and pleasure, we accepted. In September the regiment was once again formed up on parade. This time as a Royal Logistic Corps unit, the first to gain what to all intents and purpose was the freedom of a district.

The sun was shining as our Commanding Officer, Lieutenant Colonel J M Bowles MBE, led the regiment onto a beautiful improvised parade ground in the New Forest. One of the infamous New Forest ponies wandered into the area and the RQM, Lieutenant Colonel David Ferbrache, a man not to be meddled with, stepped forward, medals glinting, to usher it away. The pony, displaying a body language that suggested it too was not to be meddled with (ears down, head lowered) turned in a flash, striking out with its back legs. No one had ever seen the RQM move so fast – the RQM had never moved so fast.

The affiliation ceremony was completed with an exchange of gifts and the regiment marched past the Chairman of the New Forest District Council, with bayonets fixed, creating another small piece of history as we went.
*17 Port & Maritime Regiment*

**In At The Deep End.** 'You are not going to like this very much'. I winced as I recognised the dulcet tones of my desk officer at PB9. 'Look on the bright side, you will be right at the hub of the new Corps.' (Oh God, he is going to send me back to Deepcut.) 'And the School needs officers with the right background.' (Where is my disembowelling knife? It's the School of Ordnance. All those

THE ROYAL LOGISTIC CORPS MUSEUM   Proposal for structural improvements to existing showcases

December 1994

ABOVE: Colonel M C Sims introduces members of staff to Major General D L Burden CBE (Manning & Record Office (North), Glasgow). BELOW: Artist's sketch of typical display cabinets in the new Corps Museum at Deepcut.

years of avoiding the Ordnance Officers Course and now he expects me to teach it.) 'You will be working for a Royal Corps of Transport Lieutenant Colonel and your OC will also be a truckie.' (Forget the disembowelling knife, I will settle for jumping in front of a train. Why me, why me, why me?!) So it was that I found myself chest deep in a muddy river, at two o'clock on a cold winter's morning, dressed only in a pair of Marks and Spencer underpants. (Sorry, have I lost you? Perhaps I had better start at the beginning.)

I returned to Deepcut in October 1992 after a six year absence. Needless to say my wife was overjoyed to move back into the quarter where we had started out our married life and greeted every room like a long lost friend. ('Oh look, it's still got the toilet that you cracked and we were billed for on March Out'.) I reported for duty at the School and found that I would be working in Junior Division, which was to run, amongst other things, the new Troop Commanders and Captains Courses.

The first couple of months were frenetic to say the least. We completed the last few courses from the old School of Ordnance programme and at the same time started to bring together the skeleton training programmes for the new courses. The School of Transportation closed down and several of the staff moved across, complete with all their books and any equipment that had not been physically bolted to the floor. Offices were changed, new furniture installed and extra telephones bid for. Discussions took place on matters of grave importance: who had the best view, why has he got half a square metre more floor space than me etc. Offices were changed again and gradually things began to settle into place.

It quickly became obvious that, with the first Royal Logistic Corps course only weeks away, the learning curve for everybody was going to be pretty steep, indeed for some it was very nearly vertical. The Royal Army Ordnance Corps officers had to become familiar with the nuts and bolts of transport operations whilst,

for their Royal Corps of Transport counterparts, the news that the boxes on the back of the trucks actually contained things that had to be looked after and accounted for came as a rude awakening. Differences in terminology had to be overcome – it took me ages to work out that when people talked of sending a DR to Squadron Headquarters they meant a Despatch Rider and not a Discrepancy Report, and all had to come to grips with the outline principles of Postal & Courier, Pioneer and Catering operations.

Despite many initial teething problems things started to come together and No 1 Troop Commanders Course assembled. The climax of the course was a ten day Field Training Exercise during which the students were let loose on a real and newly formed Brigade Support Squadron. Barring the odd hiccup (one of the Royal Corps of Transport officers crashed his Land Rover) things were doing reasonably well when the Officer Commanding unleashed his master plan. 'We have done several night moves now so, just to add a bit of excitement, I thought we would make them do a river crossing tonight. I want you to supervise it. I have been through myself and, although it is a bit hairy for the Land Rovers, the 8 Tonners should be OK.'

It thus transpired that midnight found me, complete with a REME Recovery Team, standing on the bank of the river, waiting for the first packet to arrive. It was raining and the water was a muddy expanse that seemed to be moving extremely fast in the thin beam of the torch. 'What do you reckon, Staff?' I asked the REME Staff Sergeant. 'No problem, sir', he replied with a grin. 'If any of them sink, we will just hoik them out'.

Cheered by his apparent optimism I resumed my wait. Sure enough, about ten minutes later the packet arrived and, with the exception of one vehicle that turned hard right on entering the water and drove off downstream, made it safely to the opposite bank. Having rescued the lost truck I returned to the warmth of my Land Rover and was just settling down with a steaming cup of coffee when my peace was rudely disturbed by one

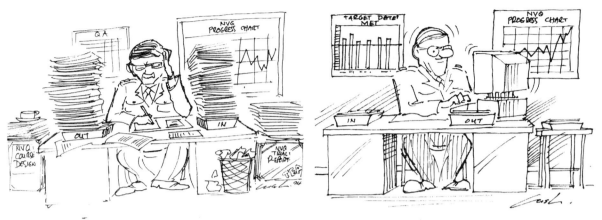

ABOVE: Before and after using database technology (School of Catering). BELOW: Final sequence of despatch from a Hercules C130 of two side-by-side 1 ton containers, on exercise in Norway (47 Air Despatch Squadron).

of my fellow instructors. 'Alright, you bloody stacker, been through yet?' he yelled uncouthly and gestured in the general direction of the swollen torrent that I had just left. 'Um, not yet. I thought I would do it later', I bluffed, not wanting to embarrass myself in front of the opposition. 'Well go on, then', he replied, 'get on with it'.

Knowing when I was beaten I started the engine and drove slowly towards the bank. 'Keep the revs high and slip the clutch'. I muttered the same good advice to myself that I had previously been issuing with such easy authority to the students. The vehicle tilted at an alarming angle and slid foward into the water. Too late I realised that the steadily rising river, which had been just shallow enough for the trucks, was definitely too deep for Land Rovers. The engine shuddered and came to a stop. A deathly silence engulfed me, broken only by the gurgling sound of water spilling in around the door. With a heavy heart I climbed out of the window and onto the roof to summon help. 'Alright, sir, you seem to be stuck', came the smug voice of the REME Staff Sergeant as he pointed out the blazingly obvious. 'Thank you, Staff', I replied through gritted teeth. 'Now what?' 'Now you get wet, sir', came the answer that confirmed my worst fears. 'I'll chuck you the line and you fasten it round one of the suspension shackles.

So it was that a pair of St Michael's finest and I ended up swimming in February. Despite my best efforts to hush things up, my fellow instructors soon found out about my misfortune and were of course deeply sympathetic. Having said that, however, I was not the only one to embarrass himself. Another member of the Directing Staff ignored the claims of a student that the future location was too soft underfoot and ended up with the better part of a troop bogged in; and of course there was the aforementioned road traffic accident. Despite these mishaps the exercise was a success and had the side-effect of welding us together, with everybody appreciating the strengths (and weaknesses) of the others. From a group of different cap badges a functioning Royal Logistic Corps team was formed.

From these humble beginnings Junior Division The School of Logistics evolved. The pace of life has slowed somewhat from those frantic early days (nowadays Tactical Exercises Without Troops and exercises are planned at least seventy-two hours before they are due to start) but the spirit remains the same. So far more than 140 Royal Logistic Corps Troop Commanders and 110 Captains Course students have passed through our doors, not to mention those from the Territorial Army, Warrant Officers, Commonwealth and Foreign Logistic Officers and Commissioning Courses. The School has become the focus for Royal Logistic Corps Doctrine and is proud of its reputation as a Centre of Excellence, training the leaders and managers for the Army of the next century.
*Walrus*

**Forging Ahead.** For the Army School of Ammunition the transition to becoming part of The Royal Logistic Corps was seamless: it was very much business as usual but with the opportunity to contribute to the success of a new and larger organisation. As an internationally accepted Centre of Excellence in all ammunition related disciplines, which attracts students from over thirty-five countries, the School has been able to advertise the existence of our new Corps around the world.

1994 saw the graduation of the first Ammunition Technical Officers and Ammunition Technicians into The Royal Logistic Corps. Graduation was marked in fine style by the attendance of our new Director General, who presented the awards. The close association between the Corps and the Worshipful Company of Gold and Silver Wyre Drawers was further cemented at the same ceremony by their presentation of a handsome decanter to the best student.

Female officers and soldiers have attended the Ammunition Technical Officers and Ammunition Technician courses for the first

LEFT: Captain Capps and Sergeant Heath receive their medals for third place in the Round London Canoe Grand Prix, 1993; RIGHT: Lance Corporal John turns on the style (11 Signal Regiment). (Courtesy of EDP Photography, Chippenham) BELOW: Sailing on a brisk close reach along the north coast of Puerto Rico, 1993 (Exercise Caribbean Wings).

time and have been quick to make their mark, a female soldier carrying off the prize for the best practical student on 1994's Ammunition Technician course.

The technical challenges posed by foreign munitions in operations in the Gulf and in former Yugoslavia have been addressed at the School through the introduction of a new training module. An impressive range of exhibits and a comprehensive foreign munition reference collection have now been established to complement the traditional training programmes.

In all respects, the Army School of Ammunition is forging ahead to ensure that it can fully meet the demands placed on The Royal Logistic Corps, both now and in the future.
*The Army School of Ammunition*

**We Sustained On Operation Grapple.** Some six months prior to the formation of The Royal Logistic Corps, 5 Ordnance Battalion Royal Army Ordnance Corps deployed on Operation Grapple to the former Yugoslavia with 17 Squadron Royal Corps of Transport under command. In April 1993 the Op Grapple 2 commitment was met by 27 Transport Regiment with a squadron from 9 Supply Regiment under command. Of significance, however, was the orbat for Op Grapple 3 as, just six months following the formation of The Royal Logistic Corps, the first multi-functional regiment of the new Corps was deployed from the UK to the war-ravaged areas of Croatia and Bosnia-Herzegovina.

4 General Support Regiment formed in Abingdon in early 1993 based on 3 Armoured Division Transport Regiment but enhanced by several different functional squadrons, including 33 Supply Squadron (formerly 33 Ordnance Company), 81 Postal & Courier Squadron (formerly 21 Postal & Courier Squadron) and 60 Squadron Royal Corps of Transport from Catterick. Soon after arrival and restructuring in its new home the regiment was warned to deploy on Op Grapple 3, this deployment to include the

Regimental Headquarters and elements of 75 Headquarters Squadron, 60 Artillery Support Squadron, 33 Supply Squadron and a significant detachment from 81 Postal & Courier Squadron.

Many lessons were learned by deploying this single multi- functional regiment overseas for the first time. Flexibility in the deployment and use of various tradesmen meant that operating procedures and general skills could be better developed, whilst the enhanced understanding and rapport between the supply and transport squadrons, which had already been developed in barracks, were easily transferred to the field, so that significant improvements to the overall logistic support effort were quickly achieved.

The excellent results of the early amalgamation of functions in a single field force regiment were clearly evident in an operational theatre. This did much to reassure the regiment itself, and the many VIP visitors to the former Yugoslavia, that Royal Logistic Corps restructuring in second line field force regiments was a highly successful operation, with clear dividends as far as efficiency and flexibility on operations were concerned.
*4 General Support Regiment.*

**1797 and All That.** Year Two for The Royal Logistic Corps and Year 200 for the Royal Yeomanry. Yes, there is a tenuous link between the two events. What of the Royal Pembroke Yeomanry and their Fishguard Battle Honour? The Pembroke Yeomanry, more commonly known as 224 Squadron The Royal Logistic Corps (V) based in Carmarthen, celebrated 200 years of the Royal Yeomanry at Windsor in the presence of Her Majesty The Queen and His Royal Highness Prince Philip. They were joined on that occasion by the rest of the Yeomanry with all their pomp and ceremony. The Fishguard Battle Honour is the only honour given for combat on British soil against a foreign power. This monumental event (if you are from Pembroke, that is) occurred in 1797 at Fishguard, where a small

ABOVE: Corps Weekend 1994. A variety of attractions. BELOW: Come
and have your face painted.

French invasion force was rounded up by the local Yeomanry and Militia, assisted by the local population.

*157 (Wales and Midlands) Transport Regiment (V)*

**Changes in Dulmen.** On 5 April 1993 Forward Ordnance Depot Dulmen became a name of the past. The signs depicting unit and sub-unit titles and the Royal Army Ordnance Corps badge were replaced with those of 14 Supply Regiment The Royal Logistic Corps.

The peacetime function of the unit has remained largely the same, the running of a materiel depot, even though it is now an alternative storage site for Donnington and Bicester. Other tasks have been taken on, namely the second line resupply of all units in Germany which are not part of 1 (UK) Armoured Division, and a mobilization role of providing a third line (rear) Materiel Supply Regiment.

The number of military posted to Dulmen has reduced, but the mobilization role and the necessary reinforcements give the regiment a war strength of some 450 men. The reinforcements are two Territorial Army squadrons, 142 Vehicle Squadron and 143 Stores Transit Squadron. Each has a Regular troop made up of Field Force soldiers employed in the base, drawn from Ludgershall and Donnington respectively.

*14 Supply Regiment*

**Flights of Fantasy.** The roar of the mighty turbo prop engines increased audibly as the huge aircraft turned to make its final approach. In the gloom at the rear of the plane, the RAF Air Loadmaster acknowledged the terse instructions which the navigator had barked over the intercom and very deliberately raised two fingers in a gesture that in other circumstances might have given offence. The Despatch Crew Commander, a Corporal, nodded briefly and then proceeded to make absolutely certain that the other three members of his Despatch Crew were aware of the two minute call. He too was on headset but the other members of his team were not and

he knew from long experince that it was absolutely vital that everyone involved knew exactly what stage they were at in the drill, especially when they were operating in darkness, after two hours low level flying. Verbal communication was practically impossible against the prevailing wall of noise as the C130 Hercules Mk 3 thundered on through the darkness towards its target. Snatching a glimpse out of the small window in the starboard paratroop door, the Despatch Crew Commander could see various light sources on the ground swaying crazily, one moment appearing to move farther away, the next looming suddenly closer as the pilot hugged the terrain at a mere 250 feet above ground level, night turned into day by the Night Vision Goggles which he was wearing.

Beads of sweat had by now appeared on the foreheads of most of the Despatch Crew. It was uncomfortably hot in the back of the aircraft, even though the night was bitterly cold outside. There had also been the exertion a few minutes earlier of removing the restraint chains from the load and then moving it carefully down the roller conveyor to its despatch station, ready at any moment to slam a chock into the roller conveyor if the aircraft had to manoeuvre suddenly. The No 3, in particular, who had swiftly and skilfully secured the final restraint, was breathing heavily from his efforts, but now, as the Loadmaster opened the ramp, a refreshing blast of cool air rushed in. All of the Despatchers stole a quick glance at the shrouded landscape which was rushing past below them, but just as quickly they focussed their undivided attention on the Despatch Crew Commander. These were the vital moments. To ensure success their actions from now on would have to be fast and precise. 'Pop up, pop up', the Navigator instructed the pilot. Some more instructions crackled over the intercom resulting in signals being made and acknowledged and the Despatch Crew burst into life. The Despatch Crew Commander and the Lance Corporal No 2

ABOVE: Captain Cowan and Corporal Spencer in the Split command
post (94 Supply Squadron, 4 General Support Regiment). BELOW:
Captain Ian Watson with the Ration Troop (33 Supply Squadron in
Bosnia).

sprang forward to remove the chocks from the roller conveyor aft of the load. By the time they had dashed forward again, the No 3 had knelt by the final restraint, his hand on the hilt of the knife which was sheathed on the leg of his flying suit.

The aircraft was by now unmistakeably climbing and the load was straining against the final restraint, which had become as taut as a bow string. 'Red On!' yelled the Despatch Crew Commander, raising his right arm vertically in front of the No 3's face, where he could not fail to notice it despite the murky conditions. The No 3 unsheathed the sharp knife. 'Green On!'. The Despatch Crew Commander's arm snapped sharply downward and the No 3 swiftly sliced through the thick cord. All of the other Despatch Crew members raced to the edge of the ramp, projecting the block of four one ton containers into the night sky. There was a series of mighty thunderclaps as the huge canopies snapped open and the Despatch Crew Commander peered intently into the gloom, hanging on to his safety belt for balance, checking for evidence that the drop had been successful. 'Four good canopies', he said over the intercom, with more than a hint of pride in his voice. 'Good job, boys, we're heading for home', said the aircraft Captain, who was a rather flashy young Flight Lieutenant, but what he could not do with a Hercules simply could not be done with a Hercules. 'These bloody Night Vision Goggles are playing up again. I cannot see a damn thing'. The DCC and Loadmaster smiled at each other. He did like his little joke.

When and where did this little scenario take place? The answer quite simply is that it could be any time and any place. Who knows when or where circumstances might dictate that the only way to get supplies through to troops on the ground is by aerial delivery? And that is what 47 Air Despatch Squadron The Royal Logistic Corps trains to do day in and day out, as well as night in and night out. When The Royal Logistic Corps was formed, very little changed for the squadron, the only unit of its

kind in the Armed Forces. Cap badge and stable belt changed of course, but the squadron's unique role working with the Royal Air Force in support of all three Services remained exactly the same as before.

The events described above did in fact take place on a training sortie dropping supplies on Salisbury Plain, but exactly the same sequence of events would have taken place if it had been on an operation.

*Major W M Carlisle, Officer Commanding 47 Air Despatch Squadron*

**NATO Rapid Reaction Corps.** Headquarters Allied Command Europe Rapid Reaction Corps formed in Ripon Barracks, Bielefeld on 2 October 1992, the initial stage in the creation of a NATO rapid reaction force designed to deploy on military operations in support of Supreme Allied Commander Europe crisis management options. In May 1994 the Headquarters moved to Joint Headquarters, the Rheindahlen Military Complex, into offices formerly occupied by Headquarters Northern Army Group.

The United Kingdom is the framework nation for HQ ARRC, and UK provides some sixty per cent of the headquarters staff plus support and communications units. There are currently a total of thirty-four Royal Logistic Corps officers and soldiers serving in HQ ARRC, with Corps personnel represented in every staff division of the headquarters, and not only in logistic staff appointments.

Royal Logistic Corps personnel also comprise the majority of the HQ ARRC Support Battalion. The battalion, which is commanded by an infantry officer, administers and trains HQ ARRC in peace, and is responsible for the headquarters' administration, movement and security on operations. The battalion, numbering some 452 officers and men, comprises 14 Squadron, 170 Pioneer Squadron and HQ Company, each commanded by a Royal Logistic Corps officer. It held its own Formation Parade in Ripon Barracks on 5 April 1993. The link with

ABOVE LEFT: Corps squash team 1993-94; RIGHT: Mountain man Captain A B McLeod climbing in the Pyrenees, 1994 (19 Mechanized Brigade). BELOW LEFT: Looking for a good view in Bavaria, 1993 (1 General Support Regiment). RIGHT: Bungee jump off the Victoria Falls Bridge in Zimbabwe (Logistic Support Battalion AMF(L)).

Bielefeld is maintained in Support Battalion's location in Rheindahlen, in Ripon Lines.

*Headquarters Allied Command Europe Rapid Reaction Corps*

**Departure of The Royal Logistic Corps from HM Tower of London.** At 1200 hours on Thursday 1 December 1994 a short ceremony and parade were held at HM Tower of London to mark the departure of the Military Ordnance (in the shape of The Royal Logistic Corps) from the Tower. Although the civilian wing of the Ordnance Department (represented by the Royal Armouries) will remain at the Tower until relocated to Leeds sometime in the near future, the departure of the Corps ends a military association going back to 1414.

The departure was marked with a parade by the Staff Band and soldiers of The Royal Logistic Corps. The parade was commanded by Captain Andy Jackson, the SO3 Catering from Logistic Support Branch, HQ London District, and the Quarter Guard formed by soldiers from 20 Transport Squadron. The Resident Governor, Major General G W Field CB OBE, Colonel Commandant The Royal Logistic Corps, inspected the Quarter Guard and made a farewell speech, after which Major General D F E Botting CB CBE, Representative Colonel Commandant The Royal Logistic Corps, unveiled a plaque outside the New Armouries building, the oldest surviving Ordnance storehouse in the country. Also on parade were four Yeoman Warders, ex-members of the Forming Corps of The Royal Logistic Corps, including the Chief Yeoman Warder, Mr Jackson, who is an ex-Royal Army Ordnance Corps Conductor.

After the parade a reception was held, during which Major General D L Burden CBE, Director General Logistic Support (Army) presented a framed Corps pennant to the Resident Governor to further mark the occasion. Colonel B E Toye, Honorary Ordnance Officer Within the Tower, and Lieutenant Colonel R Elliott, Acting Commander Logistic Support HQ London District, were also present.

*Headquarters London District*

**Logistics in Rwanda.** Operation Gabriel was the British Forces humanitarian support to the United Nations Aid Mission in Rwanda in 1994. The Commanding Officer of 5 Airborne Brigade Logistic Battalion, Lieutenant Colonel Mike Wharmby, was whisked away from Exercise Pegasus Strike along with other key players from within 5 Airborne Brigade to join the MOD recce of Rwanda on Wednesday 27 July.

After only thirty-six hours on the ground the recce team returned to Aldershot on 30 July and the requirement for a composite contingent based on 5 Airborne Brigade Logistic Battalion, 23 Parachute Field Ambulance and 9 Parachute Squadron RE was confirmed. The ensuing couple of days involved rapid repacking, kit issues and painting vehicles white. The deployment of the contingent took place under United Nations control. After much frustration the force was complete in theatre by 18 August, with 229 vehicles and towed equipments along with just under 700,000 lbs of freight on the ground in the Rwandan capital of Kigali.

Many of those employed on Operation Gabriel had little knowledge of Rwanda, other than the briefings they had received in Aldershot and the cinema footage some had viewed of Sigourney Weaver frolicking in the mountains of Rwanda with *Gorillas in the Mist*. Rwanda is a small country, similar in size to Wales but with a far more hospitable populace. It is beautifully contrasting, with areas of jungle, rain forest, mountains and volcanoes contributing to the geography. By the time we were called upon the shooting war was over, although tension within the country was high, as the Rwandan Peoples Army attempted to take control and bring an element of calm and stability to the nation.

In Kigali, the long term plan after our arrival was to occupy hard accommodation around a

ABOVE: HRH Prince Edward taking a keen interest as the 123 (Telford) Ammunition Squadron (V) team prepare to take on the fastest civilian team during a Duke of Edinburgh Award Scheme Special Project in 1994.
BELOW: A winning skill-at-arms team, with Major General D L Burden CBE, 1994 (Catering Support Regiment (V)).

sports stadium situated ten minutes from the airport. The initial intention was to build a 400 bed tented camp whilst the stadium was cleared of the appalling mess left by 20,000 refugees. The early arrival of rain soon brought a sense of urgency to the move and when the last aircraft chalk from England had arrived we were ensconced in the Amahoro Stadium with our Canadian allies. The Battalion 2IC, Maj Steve Govan, produced a new acronym for the British United Nations troops: BUNTS. Nobody plucked up the courage to inform the Canadians of their new title. The strength of the contingent was around 590, of which some 160 wore the RLC capbadge, the majority of those from 5 Airborne Brigade.

Logistic Battalion provided the contingent's HQ element and contributed substantial elements from each of the three battalion sub-units. Drivers from 63 Airborne Close Support Squadron crewed a fleet of fifty donated Bedford MK 4-ton trucks, which provided the opportunity to take part in the distribution of humanitarian stores and the return of refugees to the interior. The trucks covered 225,000 kms and moved forward nearly 1,600 tons of humanitarian stores, bringing back some 6,000 refugees. They also played a major part in the resupply of the African battalions located in the south-west of the country.

82 Airborne General Support Squadron were located in the stadium in Kigali, responsible for operating the force visibility cell as well as providing a ration section and local resource support.

As in any long stretch away from home, an efficient mail system was vital to troop morale. The speed with which the mail service was set up in Rwanda was impressive and much appreciated. As at 28 September, the two man Postal and Courier detachment from 29 Regiment had received 4,600 kg of mail and posted out over 320 kg of blueys.

9 Supply Regiment provided a team of twelve soldiers, six of whom were employed operating a bulk fuel installation holding 90,000 litres of dieso and 45,000 litres of civgas. Elements of the fuel section were also attached to the Logistic Battalion unit bulk refuelling equipment teams. They were responsible for fuel distribution around Kigali in the north of the country to Byumba, where 9 Squadron had a troop deployed, and in the south-west of Rwanda, at Kitabi where 23 Field Ambulance operated from. The balance of the detachment from 9 Supply Regiment were operating under the guise of SAS (Soaps and Suds) with the shower and laundry facility in the main administration base. PT was compulsory every day – and both services were considered essential by everyone.

The initial three weeks of the deployment saw everybody surviving on twenty-four hour ration packs of British and other national origin. Once the facilities arrived in theatre and areas were scrupulously cleaned for centralised feeding, our team of seventeen Chefs, spread across three locations, again proved their ability to provide an excellent culinary service under difficult and testing conditions.

We received a number of visitors, most notably Sir David Steele MP, Baroness Linda Chalker, Lieutenant General Sir Richard Swinburn and the Japanese Minister for Defence; needless to say Kate Adie was much in evidence during the early days of the tour but sadly she left Rwanda early in September with dysentery.

*5 Airborne Brigade Logistic Battalion*

**Army Athletics. Minor Unit Champions 1993-1994.** Base Ammunition Depot Kineton, located near Leamington Spa in Warwickshire, had a magnificent athletics season in 1993. Between May and July they won seven athletics championships at Army, Corps, District and inter-unit levels.

July saw victory in the Army Inter-Unit Team Athletics Championships, held at the Aldershot Military Stadium on Wednesday 21 July. This was the first time the unit had qualified for these finals. The Minor Units competition was a close battle throughout the day, going into the last event with only two points separating three teams. The Kineton

ABOVE: Time out in North House Street Mill, Belfast, Northern Ireland: Privates Usher, Maffon, Wagner and Matthews and Corporal Hardstaff (12 Squadron, 8 Regiment). LEFT: Lance Corporal Baston on her way to pick up President Walesa of Poland (D-Day Celebrations 1994) (41 Transport Squadron); RIGHT: Private Jackson, alias 'Fast Moving Spares', a star part of the Staff College demonstration (21 Squadron, 3 Close Support Regiment).

team, made up of young unknown talent, showed lots of grit and determination by winning the 4 x 400 m relay in an excellent time of 3 minutes 30 seconds to win the championships by a margin of four points from 12 Battery RA and eight points from 14 Regiment Royal Logistic Corps, a first for Base Ammunition Depot Kineton and The Royal Logistic Corps.

The list of achievements are: Army Minor Unit Champions, Army Minor Unit Semi-Final Winners, Wales and Western District Minor Unit Winners, London District Minor Unit Winners, RLC Minor and Overall Champions, Engineer Resources Long Marston Challenge Cup Winners

*BAD Kineton*

**Top Road Runners.** 82 Airborne General Support Squadron's running team has dominated Army and Corps running in 1994 achieving the following results: Army Minor Units Cross-Country Champions 1994, Army Minor Units Cross-Country Relay Champions 1993-94, RLC Cross-Country Champions 1994, Southern District Cross-Country Champions 1993-94, Army Half-Marathon Championships 1994, Runners-Up, Army Biathlon Championships 1994 Runners-Up.

In addition to the team effort a special mention must go to Private Felton who has won both the Army Junior and Combined Services Junior Cross-Country titles this year.

*82 Airborne General Support Squadron*

**Army and Inter-Service Triathlon Champion.** Lance Corporal Phil Kibble, 47 Air Despatch Squadron, once again won the 1993 Army Triathlon Championships, held at the Cotswold Water Park on 9 June. He completed the one-and-a-half mile swim in 20 minutes 10 seconds and moved into the lead during the twenty-five mile cycling section through the Gloucestershire countryside. There was no catching him and he reeled off

the 10 km road run in 32 minutes 50 seconds, finishing nearly two minutes clear of the runner-up.

Not content with being Army Champion, Lance Corporal Kibble underlined his overall strength by winning the Inter-Service Triathlon on 20 July at Leziate Park, Norfolk. His outstanding running ability took him away from the field in the final stage, to finish with a twenty-three second lead.

Leading the army team to victory over the Royal Marines in the Inter-Services Triathlon was Sergeant Stuart Dinwoodie, also of 47 Air Despatch Squadron, who had one of his best races of the year, finishing thirteenth overall and breaking the two hour barrier for the first time in his career. Both Kibble and Dinwoodie were selected to represent Great Britain in the World Duathlon Championshiops in Dallas, Texas in October 1993.

*47 Air Despatch Squadron*

**The Uists Relay.** To commemorate the formation of The Royal Logistic Corps here in the Outer Hebrides heads of the 'Old Corps' decided upon a sporting and social mix. The sporting side was to comprise a relay race similar in concept to the 'Dhekelia Dash' in Cyprus and the 'Stonecutter Relay' in Hong Kong and would involve fifteen RLC runners, one of whom would be an officer, another a Warrant Officer, two ladies, with the rest of the team made up of the fastest of the remaining RLC personnel in station. Each runner would complete one mile of a course starting at the operational HQ on South Uist and finishing at the regimental HQ at Benbecula, the aim being to set a target time that would be difficult for invited teams to beat in subsequent years. The social element was to comprise an Officers, Warrant Officers and Senior NCOs Regimental Dinner, a church parade and curry lunch for all Corps personnel, their families and invited guests during the weekend preceeding Formation Day and a barbeque following the relay.

*Royal Artillery Range Hebrides*

ABOVE: Tank replenishment in Canada (Logistic Training Team, British Army Training Unit Suffield). BELOW: A Postal detachment on exercise in Turkey: Captain Stewart, Private Bloor, Lance Corporal Picola (4 General Support Regiment).

**Orienteer is The Army Champion.** The 1993 Army Orienteering Championships, held in Berlin, were won by Captain Chris Sanderson, who is currently serving as an Arms Control Inspector/Interpreter with the Joint Arms Control Implementation Group at RAF Scampton. This is the first time that the army title has gone to anyone from The Royal Logistic Corps or its Forming Corps. In the meantime he collected the United Kingdom Land Forces and army titles as well as winning the day race in the Inter-Corps Championships. He also won the RAF Championships but, as a soldier, was unable to collect the prize. Additionally, he represented the army on several occasions, including on the annual tour to Sweden. His result in the Inter-Services match helped the army to another win and ensured a record sixth consecutive set of Army Colours. He has now been selected for every army team since 1988.

*RAF Scampton*

**Dulmen Marathon Trio Capture First Inter-Services Title for the Corps.** It was a case of *deja vu* at the Inter-Services Marathon Championships held at Portsmouth on 24 April 1993. The same three runners from 14 Regiment RLC in Dulmen toed the line in an attempt to retain the prestigious title of Overall Services Champions on a flattish 26.2 miles course.

The lead group of four quickly detached itself from the remainder of the 200 strong field and comprised Staff Sergeant Martin (Royal Signals), Marine Gough (RN) and Warrant Officer One (Regimental Sergeant Major) Lonnen and Warrant Officer Two (Regimental Quartermaster Sergeant) Starbuck of 14 Regiment. At twenty-one miles Warrant Officer One Lonnen pulled up sharply with severe cramp – a lack of race fitness due to his return three weeks earlier from a six months sojourn in Bosnia put paid to his chances.

The race for individual honours was now on and by the twenty-third mile the dogged Gough was dropped. So the title of Inter-Services Champion was now between Starbuck, third the previous year, and Martin, attempting to win his fourth consecutive title. The twenty-fifth mile saw Starbuck opening up a 15 metre lead on Martin but in the final mile he was overhauled by the stronger more experienced legs of the marathon specialist. Warrant Officer One Lonnen eventually 'jogged' over the line in fifth place, hotly pursued by the third team member, thirty-nine year old Lance Corporal Malone. Second, fifth and sixth places for 14 Regiment made them clear winners. They made history by winning the first Tri-Service title for The Royal Logistic Corps. As a result of two magnificent years domination, WO1 Lonnen and WO2 Starbuck were awarded their Army Colours.

**Basketball Champions.** 17 Port & Maritime Regiment have long had a tradition of being successful at basketball and last season was no exception. Early training under the watchful eye of Staff Sergeant (now Warrant Officer Two) Pask APTC and Warrant Officer Two Mick Light and entry into the local civilian league, proved to be ideal training for the army season. The team ended up as UKLF Major Unit champions, with Lance Corporal Burt being awarded the Most Valuable Player of the Competition trophy.

*17 Port & Maritime Regiment*

**The Boxing Bessey Brothers.** Lance Corporal Chris Bessey and brother Private Billy Bessey are both members of 27 Transport Regiment. Lance Corporal Bessey, having progressed from being Junior Individual Welterweight champion, Combined Services Welterweight champion and Amateur Boxing Association Welterweight champion (1993), boxed for England against Ulster on 25 June 1993. Private Billy Bessey, at 19 three years younger, has boxed heavyweight for the army against the Western Counties in Bristol, East of Scotland in Edinburgh and the Metropolitan Police. He was runner-up in the Army Boxing Championships 1993 and hopes to become the Army Champion.

ABOVE: White water rafting in Belize. Private Neil Kewn, Second
Lieutenant Neil Jurd, Corporal Darren Brooks, Privates Sammy Day and
rear left (just out of sight) Dean Skinner (24 Transport Squadron).
BELOW: Apprentices in Larnica fishing harbour before diving, 1993
(Army School of Catering).

**My Marathon Year.** For the uninitiated marathon canoeing involves racing specially designed canoes over long distances on a variety of waterways. I race for the army team, which has a strong tradition in the sport, and for Great Britain, who are World Cup holders and have the individual K1 champion.

The season began promisingly, with me racing in doubles (K2) with my partner, Sgt Alan Heath RE. The first races were the Kennet and Avon Canal based Waterside series of four events. We managed to win the first and fourth races, were placed second in number two and had a disastrous number three. The allocation of number thirteen for the race did not bode well and, sure enough, after twelve miles we broke our rudder. We could not continue on the water but had to finish the race to keep our chances of a series win alive. Solution: we ran the next seven miles along the towpath with the boat until our support crew obtained a new rudder and allowed us to finish on the river! We still managed fifth and our overall results were good enough to win us the series.

Various races followed and, flushed with success, we entered the Eindhoven International Marathon as an Army Crew. We had an excellent paddle on this eighteen mile course and finished third, ahead of a number of internationals. Someone somewhere had been impressed and we were selected to race for Great Britain at the Bosplan International Marathon in Amsterdam. In a close tactical race we raced well to finish second in a class international field.

*Captain D F Capps, 4 General Support Regiment*

**The Famous Grouse.** Our first season as The Royal Logistic Corps Cricket Club has been a great success, with the First Eleven comfortably winning The Famous Grouse Merit Table Competition and only losing one match. We also fielded a Second Eleven for a handful of matches.

This brief summary is perhaps a little deceptive. In reality the season started in March 1992 with the first planning meeting between Cricket Secretaries of the Forming Corps. At this meeting a number of decisions were taken to try to ensure that the first major team sport to represent the Corps after formation was successfully launched.

The decisions included: two sides to be organised; existing fixture lists to be amalgamated and allocated according to the perceived strength of the opposition; home fixtures to be played at Buller Barracks, Aldershot as facilities at Deepcut were not suitable and a series of pre-season nets to be arranged.

*The RLC Cricket Club 1993*

**Swords at Dawn.** Despite the depot's position as a minor unit, our 'home grown' fencers have gone from students to BAOR Major Unit champions and a return to Aldershot in May earned them the army title. The opposition, including an Olympic pentathlete and Scottish national fencer, would have frightened most, but not Sergeants Melia and Ridgeway, Lance Corporals Fallon, Cadman, Stewart, Archie Wright, Julie Wileman and Jenny Newbury. The individual results, and unit position of first with no defeats, are rewarded with a momentous trip to Earls Court and the Royal Tournament to represent the army. Who said Bracht was not a sportman's dream posting?

*3 Base Ammunition Depot*

**Exercise Island Wander 16 September - 10 October 1993.** (Extracts) At 0330 hrs we were woken by a persistent Phu who wanted us to set off well before sunrise and walk to Gorak Shep, the final village in the valley before Everest Base Camp. The walk up would be another stiff test but we hoped to be able to reach the summit of Kala Patar adjacent to Everest as the sun came up. The walk up in head torch light was almost surreal, with the ever-lightening sky casting shadows from moonlight to daylight. We hardly noticed the sheer size of the valley or the magnificence of

ABOVE LEFT: Private Merrett (33 Supply Squadron) going to the dogs in Cyprus (4 General Support Regiment); RIGHT: Private Fitton comes to grips with the smaller vehicle yard (14 Transport Squadron). BELOW LEFT: Tunnel fighting in Gibraltar (156 (North West) Transport Regiment (V)); RIGHT: Radio Troop in display formation (4 General Support Regiment).

the surrounding mountains. The steepness of the slope increased just below the snowline and a scramble over loose rocks to a small, clear ledge ensued.

The snowline was remarkably well-defined – after fitting crampons we roped up on two ropes. By now it was daylight which made the going much easier and we were also able to see clearly the route taken by the team on the previous day. The pace now was much more deliberate and the gaping crevasses very apparent. Moving like a large snake we came onto a huge snowfield above which to our left we could see the snow flutes on the ice ramp which would lead us to the summit ridge.

The lack of available oxygen combined with the severity of the slope and length of the rope to make the effort of such sustained climbing very difficult.

It was a great relief to make the final, undignified stumble onto the ridge and collapse, gasping for air. It was from there that, at about 0900 hrs, we roped up again, left our day bags and made for the summit, 500 metres to our right. The ridge is an alpine classic and by now the views were perfect. Fifteen minutes later we were at 6,189 metres (20,305 feet) on the summit of Island Peak in the Himalayas. Captain Stevens and I immediately unfurled our Royal Logistic Corps banner and became the first members of the Corps to celebrate from such a height.
*Major N F G Brehaut*

**Award of Excellence 1994.** Private Susan Dawson, aged twenty-four, has been given one of the Army's top sporting awards, the Embassy Award of Excellence, in recognition of the contribution she has made to one of Britain's more unusual sports, Women's Luge.

Private Dawson, a driver with 41 Transport Squadron in Aldershot, has always had a passion for sport and physical fitness. 'One day I just happened to be reading through squadron orders and saw a notice asking for volunteers to take part in luge training', said Pte Dawson. 'I wasn't really sure what it meant, but it sounded interesting, so I went along and haven't looked back since.'

In her first year Private Dawson won the Women's Army Novices Luge Championship and went on to take second place in the British Ladies Novices Championships in Austria in the same year. Last year she was Britain's Ladies Luge* Champion. Her sights are firmly set on representing Britain in major national and international competitions, the World Cup and ultimately the next Olympic Games.
*(Luge is the ladies bobsleigh event)
*41 Transport Squadron*

**Near the Roof of the World. World Elephant Polo Association in Kathmandu.** The idea was first dreamed up in St Moritz. Why not bring out the polo players to Nepal and play on board the elephants? So it was that in 1982 a trial was held. Those early games were played using footballs. The elephants loved it. Stamping on the balls was great sport for them, but expensive in balls. Ordinary polo balls were used and the game took off. Stamping on polo balls does the balls no harm, but hitting a well-embedded ball is difficult indeed. I was lucky enough to be in Nepal the following year when the new sport was opened to the world and to Royal Logistic Corps players, including Major Keith McGowan, our ace back and friendly Mover, and me.

So, how do you hit a polo ball from the back of an elephant? With difficulty, one has to say. Elephants, like their riders, vary greatly in size. So do the polo sticks – anything from seventy-two inches to one hundred and nine inches, or longer if you bring your own. The whippiness of the stick is also important. Some players like a firm hit, some like a good whip in the bamboo to add to the strike. Some of us are just happy to connect.

Each elephant is driven by a mahout, and each mahout is in turn driven by the player who sits on a cloth saddle, hopefully well entangled in the rope tackle. Speaking the language is a help but not foolproof. The

ABOVE: Colonel A Fisher, Commander Logistic Support London District, accompanies the General Officer Commanding The Household Division on his inspection of The King's Troop, 1994. BELOW: The Corps Mobile Display Team 1994. (Courtesy of Jim Farrar, Sandhurst)

elephants love to run with the ball and the mahouts have no tactical sense. To attract an erring elephant's attention the mahout gives it an almighty thwack on the head. To attract an erring mahout's attention, it is sometimes difficult not to emulate ...

There are simple rules to the game, which is played on a pitch some 150 x 75 metres. Four elephants make up a team, and a game of two chukkas each of ten minutes playing time takes about an hour to finish. A slow game? Don't you believe it! A running jumbo covers a lot of ground in a short time (if you are lucky). A slow elephant can be infuriating.

Games are played only in the morning, often starting when the early morning mists still obliterate the goals from the far end. Once the heat of the mid-day sun strikes, playing becomes increasingly unpleasant. Holding the stick in one hand is tiring and leaves the whole arm shaking with fatigue. The only known sure remedy for this problem is situated in a small tent at the end of the playing area.

Afternoons are spent on safari, walking in the local jungle, floating down river, or just relaxing getting ready for the evening. Players come from all over the world: the rich, the famous, and we local lads and lasses from just up the road. It's a challenge near the Roof of the World.

Don't even think about counting the cost ...
*Lieutenant Colonel R C A McAllister*

**Williamson Rugby Cup 1993.** The BOD Donnington rugby team arrived at Abingdon on 8 September 1993 for the final of the Williamson Rugby Cup (Corps Championship), with the rain falling heavily. Donnington and 17 Port & Maritime from Marchwood were the two seeded teams. Both Captains drew names out of a hat to see which half of the draw they would be in. Donnington went into the top half of the draw and played the Training Regiment & Depot . It was a scrappy game, with plenty of drop ball, but a try from Lance Corporal Jackson and a conversion from Private Wright gave Donnington a 7-0 lead which was defended

up to the final whistle. In the semi-final it was the turn of 1 Squadron of 10 Regiment to take on Donnington. The rain had stopped by now. The ball handling got a lot better and Donnington were now playing by far their best rugby. Tries from Lance Corporal Botten and Lance Corporal Jackson, coupled with two conversions and a penalty from Private Wright, gave Donnington a 17-0 victory. The two seeded teams were in the final.

Port & Maritime Regiment had the advantage in the first half with a strong wind behind them, however they could not capitalise on this and it was BOD Donnington who led 3-0 at half time, with a penalty from Pte Wright. The second half was played mainly in the 17 Regiment half, with constant pressure from Donnington leading to a try and conversion from Private Wright. Final score 11-0. BOD Donnington therefore retained the Williamson Cup for 1993. Corporal Bland received the trophy from Lieutenant Colonel (Retired) Williamson.
*Base Ordnance Depot Donnington Support Unit*

**Burst Genoas and Fast Racers.** The RLC offshore racing team sailed into the record books during the Army Sailing Association annual Offshore Regatta held in 1993. Four yachts represented the Corps in all the major racing Divisions. The skippers were Captain John Broadley (who was also the Team Manager), Major Peter Stableford, Sergeant Paul Anderson and Corporal Peter Overton. The crews came from Royal Logistic Corps units in UK, Germany and Northern Ireland.

In Division Three, with Sergeant Anderson skippering, the Victoria 34' *Mitra* was suitably guided by Corporal Stan McMillan's navigation to finish second against some strong opposition from the REME boat *Dosinia*. *Mitra's* crew were observed celebrating their success by climbing the rigging and diving into the Solent between races.

In Division Two, with Captain Broadley in another Victoria *Lambis* managed to overcome

LEFT: Captain Terry Hall — Double First at the British Veterans Athletics Federation Indoor Championships in Glasgow, 1993; RIGHT: Private Dawson, British Ladies Luge champion 1993 (41 Transport Squadron). BELOW: 1994 Corps Windsurfing team at Thorney Island. (Courtesy of EDP Photography, Stanton St Quintin, Chippenham)

equally strong opposition, again from the REME, to finish first. But then again if, as a skipper, you were forced to put up with the humour of Captains Tony Keppell-Compton and Paul Stockdale, anyone would be determined to get it over with quickly!

In Division One, the cruiser division, Major Stableford in the Corps' new BAOR yacht _St Christopher_ and Corporal Overton in another Corps yacht _Thunderer_ finished third and fourth respectively. (There is a suspicion that the sailing expertise aboard _St Christopher_ may have been diluted by the duty-frees they were carrying.) Corporal Overton, hindered by the lack of a fast boat and by the noise coming from _St Christopher_ just in front, nevertheless gave a creditable performance.

The inshore series of races was not without its moments. Burst sails (nearly all genoas) became a frequent occurrence – with the lack of a sailmaker to effect repairs between races this was a major problem. The last race in the series was the decider and therefore the pressure was immense. Just about the longest protest committee meeting in the history of the regatta was held on the Saturday night, no less than two-and- three-quarter hours. Oliver North had an easy time compared with the gruelling some of our team experienced that night before winning the protest decisions.

On the final day nobody was celebrating more than the RLCYC team. We had taken part in the Army Regatta determined to win the team prize, **The Dolphin Trophy,** to impress on the rest of the Army that The Royal Logistic Corps has arrived in strength. The Dolphin Trophy is now in our hands for the next twelve months. As this is probably the first major army trophy to be won by the Corps we intend to make a habit of winning it every year!
_Royal Logistic Corps Yacht Club Offshore Racing_

**Ski-Bob Superstar.** Lance Corporal Michelle Turner of 99 Postal & Courier Squadron stormed into 1993 with some amazing achievements.

In January she became the Army ski-bob champion and followed up this tremendous

success by becoming the British champion. Next stop was the World Championships, where Michelle gained a creditable eighth place. Back in Rheindahlen our superstar managed enough time off work to compete in the Rear Combat Zone/RAF Germany Ladies Cross-Country League and yes, you guessed it, she was a member of the winning team.

March brought a switch to judo and Michelle became the Combined Services silver medallist, having beaten the gold medallist in an earlier contest. She now goes on to represent the Combined Services in the British Championships and ultimately hopes to represent Britain one day.
_99 PC Squadron_

**The Turpin Cup.** There were a number of major changes to Army Inter-Corps tennis this year (1993). The biggest change was to the participating Corps. We have lost RCT, RAOC, RAEC, RAPC and ACC, but the Adjutant General's Corps and The Royal Logistic Corps were allowed to enter two teams, which will help to ensure that as many players as possible can play competitive tennis.

The other change is that the format of play for each fixture will comprise six singles and three doubles matches, instead of nine doubles. This has been introduced to enable our players to play more competitive single matches, as singles play forms a major part of Inter-Service matches. The honour of lifting the Turpin Cup* under these new arrangements was closely contested by the top four teams but the strength and commitment of our Corps squad proved decisive.

The Royal Logistic Corps A side amassed fifteen points during the season and in doing so remained unbeaten throughout. The only point dropped was against the Royal Artillery when points were shared in a rained-off match.

*(Presented by Maj-Gen Pat Turpin RCT, who won RASC Tennis Championships as a Lieutenant and as a Major General).
_Inter-Corps Tennis 1993_

ABOVE: Yeoman Warders escorting the VIP party to the New Armouries
in the Tower of London. BELOW: Quarter Guard from 20 Squadron on
the occasion of the Ordnance Officer leaving the Tower of London.

**Tug-of-War Inter-Service Champions 1994.** The 15 Regiment tug-of-war team was formed in April 1993. During their first outdoor season (1993-1994) the team entered as many competitions as possible, to gain much needed experience. An additional benefit was that all the hard work put in during the outdoor season paid off on the indoor circuit. This resulted in the team claiming all five weights in the United Kingdom Land Forces Indoor Championships, a feat never achieved before by any team, one of many achievements to be claimed. In December 1993 the team went on to represent United Kingdom Land Forces at the Army Championships and came away as winners in the 600 kilogrammes class, their first Army title.

The experience gained in the first year produced a much improved team at the start of the 1994-1995 season and sights were firmly set on gaining Army Colours at tug-of-war. Training at nights with Telford Tug-of-War Club, the unit team decided that our best chance of success was at the lighter weights of 560 and 600 kilogrammes. After three months training and most weekends away the team travelled to Tidworth for the United Kingdom Land Forces Championships and, after a hard day's pulling, came away as winners in the 600 kilogrammes and runners-up in the 560 kilogrammes, which allowed us to go forward to the Army finals on 2 July 1994.

During the two weeks between United Kingdom Land Forces and Army finals, the squad took three injuries - would this be our year or was fate against us? The day arrived, the draw announced; and, after long pulls against the best in Germany and UK, the team achieved their ambition to represent the Army in the Inter-Service Championships on 7 July.

The Inter-Service Championships were held at Aldershot. The squad, in their best and most confident spirit, pulled their hearts out and arms off and, after a long and tiresome day, had won the 600 kilogrammes Inter-Service Championships, the first tug-of-war title ever to be won by a minor unit and a first for the Corps. A proud Commanding Officer later presented Army Colours to ten very dedicated and determined soldiers.
*15 Regiment*

**RLC, UKLF and Army Tug-of-War Champions.** 29 Regiment has continued its notable sporting success with the 47 Air Despatch Squadron tug-of-war team. Having been formed only in 1993, a vigorous training programme has made the Air Despatchers a force to be reckoned with in what has recently been a Gunner-dominated sport. Under the relentless drive of Staff Sergeant John Cullen the team has won a string of titles at local civilian events. These served as a useful warm-up for the 1994 season of Corps, army and Inter-Service Championships, where the following results were achieved:

UKLF Champions in both 680 kg and 640 kg classes. Winners of the 680 kg class and runners-up in the 640 kg class at the inaugural RLC Championships. Army champions in the 680 kg class.

The season was rounded off in fine style when the team were invited to take part in the Royal Tournament at Earls Court in July, where they gained a creditable second place. Members of the team were all awarded army Colours for their contribution to this demanding sport.
*47 Air Despatch Squadron*

**Windsurfing in the Adriatic.** One of the classic tales of our tour in Bosnia, which reached international news headlines, was of a 'spying incident' when key members of the squadron were arrested. An idea of raising money for charity had been mooted. Warrant Officer Two (Staff Sergeant Major) Dave Mansfield hatched a cunning plan that was both enjoyable and likely to raise money for worthy causes Save the Children and Feed the Children. The idea was a sponsored windsurf along the Adriatic coast, the aim being to raise approximately £3,000. The team consisted of two windsurfers, Warrant Officer Two Mansfield and Lance Corporal Snowden, and a four man support team, with a safety boat and vehicle. The plan had been going well,

ABOVE: Major General D L Burden CBE attends the graduation of the first Ammunition Technical Officers into The Royal Logistic Corps (Army School of Ammunition). BELOW: Channel Tunnel. View of Running Tunnel showing minimal movement space and the overhead power supply (DLSA).

until the day they were resting in the back-up boat. Fifteen Croatian police, armed to the teeth, boarded the boat and promptly arrested them. The boat, being reasonably small and unable to handle the twenty people in it, began to sink. The Croatian interpreter was taken away for questioning and the remainder retreated to dry land, where they were searched and questioned. The police soon realised that, although the Staff Sergeant Major was many things, he was no James Bond. They then escorted the party back to camp, where the charges of spying were dropped. The incident not only raised money for charity, but showed the need for liaison between military and civilian authorities.
*Corporal Dick and Lance Corporal Hosie, 9 Supply Regiment*

**Finale.** These contributions in Chapter 2 come from some forty-five units and fourteen individuals. Along with other 'pieces of the jigsaw' in this book, they reflect the life of a large Corps at work and play, though no-one should think they are comprehensive in themselves. Much has had to be omitted from material available to the Editor and much more could well have been searched out for publication, but no amount of additional articles could change the overall impression of the Corps which the reader will have already gained from these pages. Another rain forest would have to be sacrificed to give a complete account but that can wait for some future historian. The Epilogue over the page, graciously provided by our Colonel-in-Chief, HRH The Princess Royal, brings to a close this look at the first two years of The Royal Logistic Corps. Subsequent years will no doubt build on these beginnings. History has to start sometime. *Editor.*

ABOVE: Preparing underslung loads on Hankley Common (63 Airborne
Close Support Squadron). BELOW: Humanitarian aid to Rwanda, 1994
(Staff Sergeant Whittaker, 63 Airborne Close Support Squadron).

186

# EPILOGUE

BUCKINGHAM PALACE

      Since I became Colonel-in-Chief of The Royal Logistic Corps on its formation on 5 April 1993 I have watched its evolution in both the Regular and Territorial Army with great interest. I and the Deputy Colonels-in-Chief, HRH The Duke of Gloucester and HRH The Duchess of Kent, have visited a broad cross-section of units in Hong Kong, Germany and throughout the United Kingdom meeting servicemen and women and civilian employees working with energy, enthusiasm and skill. We have been kept abreast of the Corps work in other parts of the World and informed of the developments designed to achieve the best value for money, in which the Corps has taken a leading role.

      My impressions after two years, are of outstanding success in meeting the challenges involved in assuming the mantle of proud traditions inherited from the antecedent corps. The Royal Logistic Corps has matured and earned respect in a surprisingly short time. This success is evident in the confident manner of the officers and soldiers that I meet; in the conduct of units on operations and in the mark that the Corps has made on the social and sporting fabric of Army life.

      I offer my congratulations for a job well done and your Royal Colonels' best wishes for the future.

Anne

# INDEX

# INDEX

# SUBSCRIBERS

## Presentation Copies

HM The Queen
HRH The Princess Royal
HRH The Duke of Gloucester GCVO
HRH The Duchess of Kent GCVO
HRH Princess Alice, Duchess of Gloucester GCB, CI, GCVO, GBE

Quartermaster General
Major General A. N. Carlier OBE
Royal Electrical and Mechanical Engineers
Adjutant General's Corps
Engineer Transport & Staff Corps
Royal Australian Corps of Transport
Royal Australian Army Ordnance Corps
Australian Army Catering Corps
Army Service Corps of India
Army Ordnance Corps of India
Malaysian Army Service Corps
Malaysian Army Ordnance Corps
Royal New Zealand Corps of Transport
Royal New Zealand Army Ordnance Corps
Army Service Corps of Pakistan
Army Ordnance Corps of Pakistan
Sri Lankan Army Service Corps
Sri Lankan Army Ordnance Corps
Worshipful Company of Carmen
Worshipful Company of Cooks

Worshipful Company of Gold & Silver Wyre Drawers
Army Museums Ogilby Trust
Army & Navy Club
MOD Library
Staff College Library
Institute of Logistics
Legal Deposit Office British Library
Imperial War Museum
National Army Museum
Canadian High Commission
Office of The Chief of Transport (US Army)
French Embassy, London
German Embassy, London
Royal Netherlands Embassy, London
US Embassy, London
Royal Hospital Chelsea
Royal Star & Garter Home
Queen Victoria School, Dunblane
Borough of Surrey Heath

# SUBSCRIBERS

Major R M Alcock RLC
Lieutenant Colonel J F J Allen MBE RLC
Captain R H Allen PSAO
Lieutenant Colonel K.B. Anderson RLC
Major M R Appleton RLC
Mr Sidney Atkins
Captain A D Baker RLC
Colonel A F Barnett OBE
Major General W Bate CB CBE DL
Mr E C Bates
Major M H Bazire RLC
Captain (QM) P J Beauchamp RLC
Major S E Bennett TD
Clive & Carolyn Birch
Mr E Bratby
CST J W Brodie, Victoria Police Band
Lieutenant Colonel P V Budd RLC
Brigadier R M Bullock CBE
Major General D L Burden CBE
Lieutenant Colonel L S Burr OBE RLC
Major N G Campbell RLC
Major General C E G Carrington CB CBE
Captain D A Carter RLC
Colonel P Chaganis OBE
Brigadier P A Chambers MBE
Mr L Christmas Ex RASC
Major General D B H Colley CB CBE
Captain G A Collier-McGirr RLC
Major G T Collinson RLC
Major R R C Cooke
Lieutenant Colonel R K Cooley late
   RASC/RCT
WO2 (SSM) J Coyne RLC(V)
Mr Erik M Crichton
24007009 WO2 K Cronin
Major E H Crossen RLC
Brigadier Y Dalby-Nash
Major M J Dalley RLC
Colonel D L Davies TD
WO1 (SSM) J Davis
Colonel R J Davy
Lieutenant Colonel H M M Deighton
Colonel C A Den-McKay OBE
Major R M Devonshire RLC
Lieutenant Colonel C J Doland
Lieutenant Colonel B S Dyson
Colonel C R Elderton OBE
Major General A F J Elmslie CB, CBE
Lieutenant Colonel J J Evans
Brigadier P A D Evans OBE
Major G W Evanson RLC(V)
Brigadier G A Ewer CBE
Lieutenant A P Fahey
Colonel C Field GM
Lieutenant Colonel N O H de Foubert RLC
Mr E B Franklin
Lieutenant Colonel P Fraser RLC
Lieutenant Colonel J S B Frere RLC
Lieutenant Colonel D N Furness-Gibbon OBE
WO1 R J D Garland RLC
Major M J Garside RLC
Colonel N E L Gilbert
Corporal D A Goodchild
Major N J Goodwin RLC
Major J J R Goût RLC

Lieutenant Colonel M J B Graham RLC
Major B O H Griffitsh TD, RLC (Retd)
WO1 (RSM) S P Griffiths RLC
Major C.J. Griggs RLC
Lieutenant Colonel M J Grinnell-Moore late
   RPC
Major J N Gunson MBE GM
Lieutenant Colonel S C Hall RLC
Lieutenant Colonel J G Hambleton MBE
Brigadier D F Harris ADC
Captain S Harrison RLC(V)
Captain S A Hawley RLC
Captain P Hepworth RLC
Chief Inspector Kenneth J Heselwood
WO1 D V Hill RLC (ACF)
Brigadier M G R Hodson CBE
Captain J S N Hornsby RLC
Major W M L Howard
General Sir Patrick Howard-Dobson GCB
Major W D Irvine RLC
Mr G Johnson
Mr P B Jowett
Brigadier R J N Kelly CBE
Major G D Kneale MBE RLC
Colonel C M Lake
WO1 A P Lambert RLC
Lieutenant Colonel T Lees TD
Major G J Leonard (US Army)
Sir Peter Levene KBE
Lieutenant Colonel J J Little RLC
Major R D Longmoor, late RAOC
WO1 (RSM) C P Longrigg RLC
Major J R Lund RLC
Captain P R Lynch RLC
Major General J D MacDonald CB CBE
Major R J Male RLC
Major D J R Martin RLC
Captain R N May BA Grad Dip Ed St,
   Grad Dip Bus, MIR
Lieutenant Colonel R C A McAllister
Captain P T McGrath RLC(V)
SSgt W E McNiven RLC
Lieutenant Colonel P D Morris RLC
Lieutenant Colonel R J Morrison OBE RLC
Lieutenant Colonel M K Murphy RLC
Lieutenant Colonel B C Neeves RLC
WO1 (SSM) G Orr RLC
Lieutenant Colonel D J Owen RLC
Lieutenant Colonel S F Owen OBE RLC
Lieutenant T J D Pemberton-Pigott RLC
Major L J Pitt RLC(V)
Brigadier A W Pollard
Captain C C Powell RASC/RCT/RLC
   March 1962 to March 1995
Lieutenant G Powell RLC
Colonel M Procter
Captain G J Pugh RLC
Colonel C J Rhodes
Cdr Gordon Rintoul, C L J
Lieutenant Colonel J D McI Ritchie RLC
Lieutenant Colonel R Rook OBE
Lieutenant Colonel R K Rowley RLC
Captain C G Russell TD, late RASC
Major V S Sanders, Hon Secretary/Treasurer
   RASC & RCT Officers' Luncheon Club

Mr Jack Schoepe FHCIMA MRSH
WO1 A R Senior RLC
Lieutenant Colonel G J Shawley TD
Captain D J D Smith RLC
Lieutenant Colonel M S Southworth RLC
Major T Tayler RLC
Major A S Taylor RLC
Lieutenant Colonel P J Taylorson RLC
Lieutenant Colonel W S Torrington RLC
Lieutenant Colonel M J Varley RLC
Colonel D B Waddell
Lieutenant Colonel E G Waite-Roberts TD
Lieutenant Colonel J E Wallace OBE, RLC
Colonel P S Walton
Major R S D Ward RLC
Captain R A M Weir RLC
WO1 T P Wellstead RLC
Colonl C H White
Brigadier W M E White CBE
Major J F G Wilberforce RLC
Lieutenant Colonel M E Wilcox RLC
Lieutenant Colonel R M Wilkinson TD
Mr D R Wood
Captain D R Woodford RLC
Lieutenant Colonel D S Wooles MBE
Captain G J Wright late RCT
Colonel G J Yeoman MBE
Colonel R York
Mr A J G Young BEM
Lieutenant Colonel M H G Young
Headquarters The Army School of Catering
4 General Support Regiment RLC
Officers' Mess, 4 General Support Regiment
   RLC
12 Supply Regiment RLC
14 Supply Regiment Officers' Mess
14 Supply Regiment RLC
14 Supply Regiment RLC Sergeants' Mess
15 Regiment RLC
27 Transport Regiment RLC
Officers' Mess, 27 Transport Regiment RLC
Sergeants' Mess, 27 Transport Regiment
   RLC
29 Transport Squadron RLC
Deepcut Detachment 41 Transport Squadron
   RLC
156 (North West) Transport Regiment
   RLC(V)
Officers' Mess, 157 Transport Regiment
   RLC(V)
234 (Wirral) Squadron RLC(V)
235 (Liverpool) Squadron RLC(V)
236 (Manchester) Squadron RLC(V)
238 (Sefton) Squadron RLC(V)
Logistic Support Regiment RLC
Army Museums Ogilby Trust
Officers' Mess, Petroleum Centre
Sergeants' Mess, Petroleum Centre
The Institution of the RASC and RCT
Sergeants' Mess, Base Ammunition Depot
   Longtown
The RASC/RCT Association
Ministry of Defence Library
Prince Consort's Library, Aldershot